Open Field

Houghton Mifflin Company   Boston   1974

John Brodie and

James D. Houston

A SAN FRANCISCO BOOK COMPANY/HOUGHTON MIFFLIN BOOK

FIRST PRINTING V

Library of Congress Cataloging in Publication Data

Brodie, John.
 Open field.
 "A San Francisco Book Company/Houghton Mifflin book."
 1. Brodie, John. 2. Football. I. Houston,
James D., joint author. II. Title.
GV939.B73A36   796.33′2′0924   74-14627
ISBN 0-913374-12-1   ISBN 0-395-19882-8

This San Francisco Book Company/Houghton Mifflin Book originated in San Francisco and was produced and published jointly. Distribution is by Houghton Mifflin Company, 2 Part Street, Boston, Massachusetts 02107.

Contents

CONTENTS

Illustrations follow page 70 and page 166

Introduction

THREE BICYCLES are stacked together on the walkway leading to his front door. We step around them out onto the grass. The lawn is wide, and there is something about the easy way he walks on it, the way a swimmer slides into water or a sailor finds his footing on the deck. All his life this has been John Brodie's natural habitat — ball fields, golf links, the city park he grew up in, his own spread of mowed lawn — these flat expanses of green California grass.

He ushers me inside. It's a big, elegant house, with fine rugs and a good piano, but not the kind of elegance you're afraid to touch or sit down on — because it is a house full of kids. The Brodies have five — ages sixteen, fourteen, twelve, ten, and two. And they roam the house at will. During one day we spent taping his recollections, four of them were all home at once, with colds, in robes and pajamas. The youngest, towheaded Erin, kept wandering into the room where we had set up the mike. She wanted to be next to Daddy, and she was intrigued by the machine. We have some of her comments recorded, somewhere between John's account of the Oakland game in 1970 and the Detroit game in 1971. The fine thing was that John never broke his stride. Picking up and cuddling his two-year-old was just as natural as remembering a battle of wits waged against the meanest linebacker in the league. It was nice to see.

At ease in his den, in his golfer's cardigan, with his two-year-old on his knee, it's hard to believe he spent seventeen years of his life in that risky arena with the likes of Dick Butkus, Big Daddy Lipscomb, and Alex Karras aiming to fold him double. His handsome Irishman's good looks are deceptive. He seems younger than his thirty-eight years. His shoulders slope forward so that you don't notice their size unless you're looking for evidence. His tanned face is so open, so mobile it takes a while to notice the ballplayer's neck, which is as wide as his face and even wider at the collar.

This is the quarterback Clark Shaughnessy called one of the two greatest passers in professional football. In 1971, Tom Landry, head coach of the Dallas Cowboys, said, "The highest tribute that can be paid a quarterback is to be able to say that he strikes a little fear into whatever defensive team he faces. Brodie does that. I marvel at the way he has now mastered the art." Meanwhile his hometown fans booed him steadily for a decade. "The 49ers ain't ever going to win a championship as long as Brodie runs that team," you would hear from the stands, and from the barstools, and from the living rooms of San Francisco.

As of December 1973, his controversial career as a player ended. But Brodie is not one to sit back and savor the success that came to him so abundantly in his final

viii

years. Nowadays he is more active than ever. During the month in which we did most of the taping, he flew to Washington, D.C., for a conference on ways to improve and standardize artificial turf; he played in the San Francisco City golf championships; he signed with NBC–TV as their color commentator for the fall football season; he appeared at two or three fund-raising banquets; and he drove to Sacramento where he is helping to expand a branch of the drug abuse prevention program he's very much involved with. A teen-age cousin of his was staying with the family at the time, taking part in this program in Palo Alto, where John is the local director. Several mornings he excused himself for half an hour while he drove his young cousin to the downtown center.

In the midst of this kind of schedule we began to gather his memories and anecdotes, his feelings and conclusions after half a lifetime inside the pressure cooker that is a quarterback's world. His range of experience is extraordinary. In the century or so of recorded football history, only a handful of men have put in as much active playing time — twenty-four successive seasons, from his first high school scrimmage to his final professional game. Yet the story that emerges is not that of a man "in retirement," summing up the past. Rather, it catches him in midstride — one of the most formidable strategists ever to play the game, stopping just long enough to tell us how he survived it, what he learned, and where he is headed next.

JAMES D. HOUSTON

Santa Cruz, California
May 1974

This book is dedicated to my mother,
MARGARET BRODIE,
and to the memory of my father,
ALOYSIUS LEO BRODIE,
with deep gratitude.

MANY PEOPLE contributed to the making of this book, more than can be acknowledged here. But special thanks are due to Y. A. Tittle, for freely sharing his memories and opinions; to Bill Nichols of the *San Francisco Examiner* for access to his excellent photography; to the San Francisco 49ers management and public relations staff for their cooperation throughout; and most of all, to the hundreds of athletes I have had the privilege of playing with and against.

PROLOGUE: MAKING CONTACT

LIFE IS NOT like a football game. But by playing football you can learn a whole lot about life. I know this much: neither one of them starts at the beginning. The groundwork is being laid long before you appear on the scene. I was an athlete before I was a football player. Don't ask me why I was an athlete. I just was.

The first time I played football I was fifteen years old, a long, bony sophomore, new to the school. I didn't much like the look of the game and half hoped I wouldn't last very long out there. Before I left junior high my P.E. teacher, Stu Carter, who had seen me throwing a ball around the playground, told me I could probably make first string at Oakland Tech. He said I could already throw better than anyone he had seen over there. That's why I had turned out for the team. I was flattered. I felt obliged to live up to his opinion of me. The next thing I knew I was four yards behind the line of scrimmage, being pushed and shoved and mauled and pawed at and knocked back on my can by a gang of what I considered at

1

that time to be burly linemen, all two and three years older than I was and seemingly bent on leaving me dismembered for life. I kept listening for my bones to snap, expecting unbearable pain. Then everyone was climbing off, like a game film running in reverse. I got up and looked around and settled my shoulders and patted my thighs, as if for the hell of it, but actually feeling to see if they were still there, and I said to myself, "That's not as bad as I thought it was going to be. That didn't hurt so much. Maybe it looks a lot worse than it really is."

The hitting was something I'd had no experience with. I wasn't a tough kid, did not think of myself as someone who ought to be able to "take" this kind of assault. It took me a year to get used to the hitting. But after that season I seldom gave it more than a glancing thought until 1971, the first time I got tackled hard on artificial turf at Candlestick Park in San Francisco. Even then I didn't mind the tackle. It was what I landed on — which might have been a shade softer than a basketball floor. It's a funny thing how so many people who watch football think the hardest part of being a quarterback is that physical danger you seem to be in every time the ball is snapped and anywhere from 1000 to 1500 pounds of malice come trying to trample you under. I have never looked forward to getting hit. I just took it for granted, an occupational hazard. For almost the whole time I was playing, I really didn't think about that part of it at all.

I've thought a lot about the rest of it though. In the years between high school and Candlestick, I've mulled through almost every aspect of a quarterback's world, from where I want the laces when I take the ball from center to how this line of work could help me lead a fuller life, or hinder me. By the time I left football, quarter-backing had provided me with a great education. I had found a way of being me and being in the world that I value very much. It's one reason I finally learned to love football, and love it now.

What in the Hell
Am I Doing Here?

1 I SAY *learned* to love football be-
cause I spent the first five of those years deciding whether
or not I even liked to play. I started several years later
than most of the kids I grew up with. Maybe I was that
far behind in my development. Or it may have been that
I was good at several sports in school and there were
others I enjoyed a whole lot more. Basketball, for instance. I was much more relaxed playing basketball. I
knew more about the game. Across the street from our
house in Oakland there was a hoop where I'd been working out since I was eight. It's a game you can excel at
early, if you have your coordination. Baseball and tennis
were two other sports I naturally took to. I grew up right
next to Montclair Park. I might as well say I grew up *in*
Montclair Park. During my grammar school days my
younger brother, Bill, and I lived there. We were over
there every afternoon. By the time I entered Oakland
Tech High, in 1950, athletics had become my one and
only interest in life. But at Oakland Tech, no sport could
compete with football when it came to prestige. Once I

5

made the team, that was the main reason I stuck with it. I liked the notoriety. I liked to be seen walking down the hall in my block sweater.

That first year, as a tall, rickety, tenth-grade newcomer, I also reveled in the association with the older guys who were already heroes in the school. Actually it was a lucky place to start playing football. Thanks to coach Gil Callies, an inspired, warm-hearted disciplinarian, there was a nucleus of eight or ten first-rate players who went on from there to excel in college and pro ball — an exceptional gathering when I think back on it. A quarterback in high school, Pervis Atkins, later starred at halfback with the Los Angeles Rams and the Oakland Raiders. Charlie Hardy played end for three years at San Jose State and went on to join the original Raiders team. Proverb Jacobs was an All-American lineman at Cal, then played with the Philadelphia Eagles and other pro teams before returning to Cal as a coach. And Doug Peters, who was as good a friend as I had in high school, went on to UCLA (where, as I will go into later, he played a role in a game that permanently changed my attitude toward football), then spent a few years in the Canadian League. Doug was a year ahead of me, a huge, tough-running fullback who sort of took me under his wing.

These were some of my teammates at Oakland Tech, and off the field I loved their companionship. On the field, especially during my sophomore year, I spent most of my effort trying not to expose my fear. During a game I would sit on the sidelines pretending I wanted to get in, and dreading the moment the coach would call my name. The violence didn't trouble me as much as my own confusion. I never knew quite what the hell I was doing or

6

was supposed to be doing out there. I played whenever they wanted me to throw the ball. When it was time to run, Callies would pull me out. He was trying to protect me. I had grown nine inches between eighth and ninth grade, had beanpoled up to 6-1, and weighed in at a booming 125. In the first scrimmage of the year I had tried to straight-arm some guy — imagining I was Jackie Jensen, the great Cal fullback — and I broke my wrist. That's how skinny I was.

They fixed me up with a brace, and I played out the season. But it wasn't much fun. Just getting the team grouped into a huddle would throw me into a prickly sweat. I don't know what I expected them to do after we had finished a play, but somehow I never really believed any of them would be there, or would be interested in hearing whatever I was going to say next. Each time we got grouped up, it would surprise the hell out of me. If I could accomplish that and call out some play or another in my artificial baritone, and clap my hands to break the huddle, the way I thought inspired quarterbacks were supposed to do, I felt I had done my job. As I turned to face the opposing team, it usually came as an alarming shock that there was still the play to *execute*. I would throw balls all over the field, on impulse, at random, to whoever was running and looked like he might get into the clear.

Somehow we took the Oakland Athletic League championship — the first time Oakland Tech had won it in about fifteen years. In fact, we won it two out of the three years I was there. And as I said, I liked all the glory and the attention that came along with winning. But I never really liked the game in those days. I didn't understand it

7

yet, and obviously I was playing it for a lot of the wrong reasons.

I did learn one invaluable lesson in high school. When I was a junior we were playing Oakland High. Sometime during the second half, Coach Callies put me in. I called two pass plays and he pulled me right back out. I don't remember why. That was my entire contribution for the afternoon. Two plays. But after the game the officials selected me Most Valuable Player. In our league they didn't keep very close tabs on who was playing what, or how, or when. I remember laughing with embarrassment when I heard the announcement, and the coach saying, "What the hell. Go on. Get it. They awarded it to you. What the hell." He was kind of amused by it too. So I accepted the award as the most valuable player in the game against Oakland High, and I kept that honor in mind for the rest of my career. It helped me survive some rough seasons when I thought I had played as well as ever and no one seemed to notice. And it helped me keep my head straight when, in another year, they told me I had made All-American or All-Pro. Don't misunderstand me. I loved getting those awards as much as anyone would. But after the Oakland game, when I was sixteen, I never quite trusted the awards or the ability of the awarders, and I saw how important it was to have my own personal system for evaluating whatever I had done or failed to do.

When I entered Stanford in 1953 I hadn't changed much, except on the scales. I was beefing up at a regular rate of ten pounds per year. I arrived weighing 165 and weighed 200 when I left, which is about where I've stayed ever since. I was still going out for several sports, with football on my list, but not first by any means. My senior year at Oakland Tech I made All-City in basketball. In baseball I hit .400 and made second string All-City as a fielder behind Frank Robinson, who had graduated that same year from McClymonds High, across town. In football I hadn't done so badly. I made third string All-Northern California. Before I left, Coach Callies had strongly encouraged me to play baseball and basketball in college, but he never said much about my football future. I got the impression that he wanted me to concentrate on what he figured were my strongest assets.

At the time he was absolutely right. His attitude had nothing to do with my ability to pass or to take a lick. He had observed something in my personality. Football takes a hypertense involvement. Some people would say a kind of fanatic involvement. I don't think he saw enough of that in me. He knew that in college the game changes drastically, and a player can only get so far on his arm or his speed.

In high school, football genuinely had been a *game*. At Stanford it was an institution, composed of traditions, myths, legends, interconference rivalries, coaches' reputations, student body, alumni, booster clubs, and various administrators concerned with the financial future of the campus. To survive the pressures all this brings to the playing field, a player had to care a great deal about it, he had to believe in it, or somehow convince himself that football was worth the effort. At least, this was my experience. I wasn't getting any money for playing at Stanford. I wasn't on an athletic scholarship. (It has been written that I turned one down, but the truth is, they never of-

fered me one.) There was no reason I *had* to play football. The only pay I got in those days was what the game
itself had to offer. In the long run, I think this was an advantage. It simplified, or you might say it purified, the
struggle. What I had to come to terms with was the nature of the game itself and the question: Did I like it well
enough to play it? This, in turn, served as an early preparation for what I'd have to deal with during all my years
in professional ball, where the pressures continue to mul-
tiply, in proportion to the cash investment, and the game
itself sometimes seems totally forgotten, lost, buried
under the mountain of contracts, drafts, trades, mergers,
zoom lenses, Rolleiflexes, instant replays, sponsors, press
conferences, and statistics.

In 1953 the freshman team had a two-game season. I
shared the starting quarterback spot and ended up playing
most of both games. A few months later I turned out for
spring practice, the same way I had turned out for basketball and would later turn out for golf. The varsity quarterback was graduating that spring, which left the position
up for grabs. When I found this out and saw I might actually have a shot at it, I started hustling. For a while I got
very excited. I have always enjoyed having a go at that
kind of clear-cut competition. Mentally, though, I was
still uncertain, constantly wavering in my feelings about
the game. Chuck Taylor, who was head coach then, sort
of forced my hand by sending me an incredible and entirely unexpected letter soon after classes ended in June.

John, he wrote, *your improvement between the freshman season and spring practice has been so great, if you
continue to develop at this rate, with your abilities,
there's no telling how far you can go. The way we see it*

10

now, we plan to start you at quarterback next fall. This is just to prepare you for that, and give you a chance to begin getting ready.

I was up in Hayden Lake, Idaho, at the time, where my mother had been raised. I was stunned. I was also dismayed. My first thought was, "Shit! Now I *have* to play football!"

Chuck was probably the only college coach I could have played for at that time. He allowed me to see football the way I did. He did not like the way the sport had been institutionalized. He wasn't a high-pressure coach, he just brought a lot of enthusiasm and positive thinking to the job. "What the hell," he would tell me, "just go play 'em. It ain't your life, ya know. It's only a game, for Christ sake."

When his letter came, it was like the compliment I'd received from Stu Carter in junior high. It became a kind of obligation to live up to the faith he was showing in me. By the following fall, my second year, I was starting at quarterback with the Stanford varsity.

We won the opener against College of the Pacific, 13-12. Then we played Illinois and beat them, 12-2. They were the number-two-rated team in the nation — with J. C. Caroline, the two-time All-American at halfback — and slated to win everything that year. When we came out of nowhere to beat them, well, we instantly started thinking to ourselves, "Hell, if Illinois is number two, and we beat Illinois, doesn't that make us number one?"

We just didn't know any better. When we went up against Oregon the following week, we beat them too. If we'd known more about what we were doing, we would've realized, from the way we played, that this kind

of thing couldn't last. I couldn't really blame the Oregon
fans for the way they almost trampled us after the game. I
would have felt the same way myself. They had George
Shaw at quarterback; a year later he went to the Baltimore
Colts as the first college draft choice in the country.
Those people in Oregon thought they were on their way
to the Rose Bowl.

Here's what happened. With three minutes to go we
were behind 13-12, and up to that time we hadn't done
anything to brag about — one score on a recovered
fumble, one score on a long pass. When we took over the
ball on our own thirty-five, I looked at John Stewart, our
lanky, 6-5 receiver, and asked him what he could do.

"I don't know," he said. "Just throw it on down there.
I don't even think they're watching me."

So I called it, and by the time I got the ball off, John
was eight yards in the clear. George Shaw, who played
safety on defense, saw the ball coming, and he started for
it, running toward John, with his back to me, so that the
ball, which I had thrown a little short, hit Shaw on the
helmet, bounced off, and shot forward another five yards
right into the arms of John Stewart, who caught it on the
dead run and took it in for the winning score.

From that point until the final gun the whole place was
in an uproar. The Oregon team was totally frustrated at
having been beaten by anybody, and especially by Stanford, on such an off-the-wall play. Half-a-dozen players
were fighting on the field. As soon as the gun went off,
the crowd, instead of heading up the aisles toward the
exits and the parking lots, started oozing down out of the
stands, converging on the ballplayers. This was Multnomah Stadium, which is built like a fishbowl, with the

12

players' exit halfway up a ramp in the middle of the stands. There was no way out, except through the crowd.

Pretty soon we were all bunched together, like a wagon train in Indian territory, wondering what the hell we were going to do, and Chuck Taylor had an inspiration. He pushed his way over to a microphone and announced through the PA system, "OKAY. I'VE HELD THESE GUYS BACK AS LONG AS I CAN. IF YOU PEOPLE DON'T CLEAR THE AREA IN TWO MINUTES, I'M GOING TO TURN THEM LOOSE!"

There were forty of us and about twenty-five thousand of them. But somehow it worked. At least, a kind of path started to open up. We eased through the crowd, toward the ramp, surrounded by resentful Oregonians still spoiling for some action. I had just started up the ramp when I came upon a pregnant woman who had fallen somewhere up above me and came tumbling down in my direction. I bent over to pick her up, and just as I did, her husband appeared and took a swing at me. For touching his wife. I said, "Jesus, pal, I'm just helping this gal out. She's getting stepped on."

Jerry Gustafson, our other quarterback, was right behind me. He came to my defense. "Hey, man, he's just trying to give the lady a hand." So the husband belted Jerry and almost knocked him out.

Nobody had been hurt at the end of the ball game, but by the time we got back to the locker room we could have used an ambulance or two.

Those were my first three games in college ball. As long as we were winning them, I was having a pretty good time. I could laugh about the near massacre in

13

Multnomah Stadium. It was when we started losing that I got into trouble. Like the team as a whole, I had come through the first three games with a false sense of my own ability. We were a young team. We didn't know how good we were, or how bad we were. I didn't really know why we had won, so I wasn't very well prepared to cope with the losses.

In the fourth game we played UCLA and they ran right over us, 72-0. The same thing happened when we played Navy. For the second game in a row we didn't score a point. After one disastrous play, during the fourth quarter of that Navy game, I came wheezing back to the huddle and saw all my bedraggled and beaten teammates waiting for me to say something. Nothing is more demoralizing than the last quarter of a game, when you know you haven't got a chance. I had been playing both offense and defense, and I was so tired I didn't know what to say or what play to call. Suddenly the whole idea of playing football, of putting myself through this kind of crap, made no sense to me at all. I imagined myself in a polo shirt teeing off down a close-cropped fairway. I imagined myself driving down a glistening hardwood court, in the clear, and rising to the net for a perfect lay-up. But here I was in the middle of Stanford Memorial Stadium, with twenty-one men and forty thousand fans waiting for me to call the next play and I was looking at my shoelaces thinking, "Just what in the hell am I doing here?"

The question itself was one of the reasons we were behind that day. I was calling plays, but my full attention wasn't on the field. Too much of it was on my uncertainties. I had lost the incentive that drove me to make first string. Maybe *knowing* I could do it was enough. Doing

14

it was something else again — playing hard and well all season, game in and game out. It was ironic. Athletics was my whole life, my only real interest, yet playing football was not a satisfying experience, and I could not fathom why, of all the sports I played well and enjoyed, this had turned out to be the one that was now taking up all my time.

Two games later I was sitting on the bench. When my junior year started I was still sitting on the bench, watching Jerry Gustafson run the team. For four games I watched him call plays while I sat mulling over my motives for suiting up at all, embarrassed to be on the sidelines and kicking myself for being paralyzed by such stupid indecision. I liked Jerry, he was a good athlete and a smart quarterback who got along well with the guys. But I knew I was a better thrower, which was what the team needed to spark a winning offense. We'd never get very far running the ball that season, we had to throw the hell out of it. I knew that Chuck would be starting me if I were willing to play up to my ability. What was worse, all the guys on the team knew it too. Each time I didn't play I felt I was letting them down, out of sheer reluctance to go all out.

Sitting through most of those four games I had a chance to look at myself pretty closely and weigh my choices. It was my first bout with something I'd be wrestling with, in one form or another, throughout my football career: responsibility. At this point, it was my own unwillingness to take a greater responsibility for what was happening out there on the field, to care enough to do that, and to show enough strength to handle the added pressures of collegiate football. If I couldn't do that, I might as well

15

quit playing football altogether. Anything in between —
like this benchwarming routine — was a waste of everyone's time.

If Chuck had kept me on the bench for the rest of that
season — and he had plenty of cause to justify it — my
football career might have had an early end. But by an
amazing stroke of luck, just about the time I reached this
point of decision, I had a chance to put myself to the test.

It was during the game against UCLA. By the end of
the first quarter we were behind 21-0. Chuck pulled
Jerry out and put me in, probably figuring things couldn't
get any worse than they already were.

"Brodie!" he yelled.

"Yes, sir!"

"Get in there!"

"Yes, SIR!"

I was ready. For the first time in a year, I was excited
about going into a game. I knew that if I was ever going
to play football, if I was ever going to test what I was
made of, today would be the day. There were two
aspects of the situation on the field that added to my enthusiasm. First, my old high school teammate and men-
tor, Doug Peters, was playing tailback for UCLA. During
the first quarter I had been watching him, wishing I could
perform a little for his benefit. In high school, at
around 210, he had seemed awesomely large. He hadn't
grown much in those three years. Now, in college, he
was just an average-sized back. In fact, it was sort of com-
forting to see Doug out there among all the anonymous
faces. One difference between college and pro ball, in
the pros you see the same faces season after season, you
get to know certain players extremely well. In college

16

you come up against a man once, sometimes twice, and that's it. The opposition always seemed to me rather faceless. Doug's presence that day, his familiar face, was relaxing. It loosened the atmosphere.

This, together, with the score, somehow freed me of all the pressures I had placed upon myself in other games. The score made it pretty clear that there was no way we could win it. UCLA was a top team in the nation, while Stanford was barely an also-ran. The previous year they had beaten us, 72-0. Today they were favored by four touchdowns. With the score 21-0 after only one quarter of play, winning it just didn't enter my mind. I was going to play for the sake of playing itself.

I began throwing the football like I never had before. I was firing passes all over the field. I found myself running with the ball. I had never been much of a runner. I didn't know how to run, and when I did, my main concern had been to avoid getting my bony body broken in half. That afternoon I thought to myself, "The hell with it." I started scrambling. It felt great.

But the most exciting part was the way the field itself opened up, giving me my first glimpse of how a quarterback really has to see the game in order to make it a creative experience rather than a merely technical or mechanical one. Midway through the third quarter, for example, we had the ball on about their thirty-five-yard line. It was third down and seven, and I called a pass play, intending to throw out to the sideline. When we got to the line of scrimmage I saw their outside linebacker jump forward into a hole in the line, and what popped into my mind was the route Paul Camera, our right end, was going to run, behind the space vacated by that line-

17

backer. I had never thrown a ball to that receiver on that pass play, not even in practice. The truth is, until that moment, I had never really understood the whole purpose of the play or why that particular route was part of it. When that linebacker jumped, the play's whole pattern clicked into focus.

As I dropped back, Paul came lollygagging down the middle, figuring no one was even looking at him — since no one ever had — and when I hit him with the ball he was the most surprised man in the stadium. It didn't rattle him. He picked up about twenty-five yards, ran it down to their ten, and set up our second touchdown.

That was the way it went the whole afternoon. Instead of using rote responses I had picked up in the chalk talks, I was responding to what was forming right out there in front of me. In addition to thinking about what the play should be, or what play I should call in such and such a situation, I could think about where we wanted the ball to be located on the field; and for the first time I was intensely aware of the other team's personnel. I was actually *looking* at them for signs of fatigue, for little wrinkles in their defense.

I completed something like seventeen out of twenty-one passes. Our whole team caught fire. By the final gun the score was 21-13, and we had the ball on UCLA's one-yard line. A team like ours! The also-rans. It was the most fun I'd had in my entire life. The enjoyment of playing well, and at a new level, had superseded all the drudgery. I had really been after it that day, and I had uncovered abilities I didn't even know I had. I thought, "Now I know why I play this game." I had discovered that I *could* play it. From that point on I understood the importance of getting mentally prepared. I knew then why you can't go into a game in a superficial frame of mind.

After UCLA our team had a 1-3 record. Five games later it was 6-3. That game had turned the season around. It also turned me around. For the rest of that year, and all of the next, I started at quarterback. At the end of 1956 I was selected for the All-American Team. I hadn't forgotten the award I'd received for being the most valuable player in the Oakland game. I was still watchful of awarders. So was Chuck Taylor. Before we flew back to play Ohio State, for the third game of the season, he told me that a lot of influential midwestern and eastern sportswriters would be watching this game closely.

"No matter what you do out here on the West Coast," he said, "it's the people back there who pick the teams. Until you've done it in Ohio, you haven't done it. If you have a good day, well, let me put it this way, it won't do you any harm."

Ohio State was the top team in the country in 1956. They had Jim Parker, the All-American tackle who later ended up in the Football Hall of Fame, plus four other guys who went on to play well in the pros. We were still licking our wounds from a game the previous week against Michigan, a real, old-fashioned shit-kicking that left us short eleven men. Back in Ohio, Migs Jones, who had been our third-string guard, found himself starting his first college football game, pitting his 195 pounds against Parker's 260. That's how outmanned we were.

The forecasters figured us to lose it by thirty points. We only lost by twelve — 32-20 — and I think I hit twenty-five out of thirty-two pass attempts that afternoon.

19

As Chuck had predicted, dozens of writers were following the game. When I made All-American a couple of months later, I attributed a lot of it to the coverage in Ohio. I had some good days that season — in fact, we came within one point of a shot at the Rose Bowl — and some not so good days. They happened to see me on a day when I couldn't miss. At least four other quarterbacks playing their final year of college ball could have made it: Sonny Jurgensen, Milt Plum, Len Dawson, Paul Hornung. I was pleased, of course. Who wouldn't be? Still, I saw it as a fluke. There were so many ways it could have gone.

According to the papers, making All-American was the climax of my college career. In terms of public recognition I guess it was. For me, though, the peak moment had come a year earlier, the day we almost overtook UCLA and I discovered how exhilarating football can be when you're ready to play and willing to go out and just play the game itself. A person can *tell* you that and keep telling you that, as Chuck Taylor had tried to tell me for two years, but only after I discovered it for myself did the game open up for me.

Getting Educated

2 I DIDN'T THINK ABOUT professional football until my senior year. But all along I had figured athletics was going to be my life and livelihood, one way or another. During four years at Stanford, you might say I went out of my way not to prepare myself for much of anything else. At the time it seemed perfectly appropriate to me that during my last month there I signed my first contract with the San Francisco 49ers and was expelled from the university for cheating on a test.

That I had been admitted to Stanford at all is something I have to thank my mother for. Without her efforts and encouragement, I would never have made it and thus might never have had the chance to play for a major university.

As for my state of mind as a student, well, to explain that, I have to explain a few things about my father.

He was an extremely sensitive yet tough-minded midwesterner of Scots-Irish descent. In high school, and later at the University of North Dakota, he was an outstanding football and basketball player. After college he went into the insurance business and eventually headed west. He met my mother in Seattle, where she had stayed to work after finishing at the University of Washington. The insurance business brought them down to California a few years before I was born in 1935.

In the midforties he teamed up with a group of physicians in northern California and "made it," establishing what came to be known as the Kaiser Foundation Health Plan. It originated in our living room, with my mother at the typewriter, and my brother, Bill, and I licking what seemed like thousands of stamps for all the mailers Dad was sending out. He was a man of great imagination, forever dreaming up plans and schemes. This happened to be one that he followed through on, and it clicked.

He was also the wisest man I have ever known. He used to have the habit of sitting out by an old oak tree behind our house. He would take along a little something to drink, and he would sit out there by himself for hours, thinking. Bill and I would join him from time to time, usually one or the other of us, because Dad enjoyed our company, liked to have us sitting around with him like that, and we would talk about all kinds of things. We could ask him about our personal problems, or listen to him philosophize about whatever was on his mind.

Once when I was about ten years old I was sitting with him out by the oak tree and he started talking about professional football. "In another twenty years," he said, "football is going to be one of the biggest things in the world. Instead of making ten thousand a year, quarterbacks are going to be making sixty and seventy thousand. Teams are going to be playing in fifty-thousand-seat stadiums, and the players are going to be taking the place of movie stars.

22

"I could be wrong, John," he went on, "but I know that people are looking more and more for something real to relate to outside their own lives, something they can enjoy, and the most real thing I know of is athletic involvement."

I didn't know what he was talking about at the time. If I had, I probably would have figured he was nuts. In 1945 pro football was about as profitable as Rugby.

He knew what he was talking about, of course. He had been following athletics avidly all his life. After he quit playing, he became the ultimate sports enthusiast. He used to take us to all kinds of athletic events. When Bill and I reached the age where we could start to throw a ball around, he did everything he could to encourage us to play. He didn't push us into it, he just allowed us to go as far as we wanted to in that direction. He never stressed academic achievement. He wanted me to get good grades, but mainly so that I could keep going out for sports. Dad believed that sports was a pretty good school in itself.

When I was fifteen or sixteen we were sitting out by his tree one evening and the subject of education came up.

"An education takes place," he said, "when you can apply what you have learned to a specific area. And in so many cases in higher education, there is no application for whatever it is you have learned. So a lot of people who are educated in universities have to unlearn what they learned there, after they get out, in order to begin functioning in the world. You are an athlete first and foremost, so my advice when you go to college is to be the best athlete you can be. Meet people. Enjoy yourself. When you're learning a subject, envision the application

23

of it. Absorb things you think you can truly apply to the rest of your life."

This was advice I was glad to have. At Stanford I simply was not ready for most of what went on in the classrooms. I had not prepared myself to go to college, and I was totally overwhelmed. It wasn't that my high school grades were bad — they were actually pretty high — but if there was something happening in high school that was supposed to prepare one to cope with college, I had overlooked it. My reading comprehension was pathetic. In any good-size paragraph there would be six or seven words I didn't understand. And I didn't know, then, where to begin to improve this situation. For one thing, I had never learned how to learn. The truth is, fifteen more years would have to pass before I was ready or willing to learn about matters not directly related to athletics. At age thirty-five I reached a crisis in my personal life where a lot of things I did not know finally caught up with me. I reached a point where playing better football and living a healthier life both depended on the same thing: changing the way I thought and felt and even perceived the world. Then I started learning fast.

But at Stanford I was the classic jock. I studied history because it required the lowest number of units to complete the major. I put off Freshman English until my sophomore year, hoping I'd have a better chance to unravel its mysteries. This didn't improve my grade much, but it was a lucky delay. I met my wife in that English class. She was right on schedule, taking the course as a beautiful, blond, and bright-eyed freshman from Woodland, California, up in the Sacramento Valley. She was also wearing an engagement ring. Since I myself had recently severed the tie with my old high school girl friend and was still recovering from that, we didn't do much more than chat, until the night I met her father at a postseason football banquet.

He is a physician and a Stanford alumnus. He knew I was the sophomore quarterback, and after the banquet he came up to me and said he understood his daughter and I were in the same English class. When he described her, I said, "You mean the girl with the ring." And he said to me in an offhand way, "Oh, I wouldn't worry about *that*."

It turned out that he wasn't very excited about Sue's getting married at that age, and by then neither was Sue. This is what can happen when you go away to college. Not too long afterward I asked her out.

We went together for the next two years. She was with me in Las Vegas when I got news of my expulsion. This was June of 1957. We were on our honeymoon by that time, spending my bonus money, and we laughed about the headlines in the San Francisco papers.

A few days earlier it hadn't seemed so funny. The thing was, I didn't cheat on the test everyone was so worried about. It was a movie appreciation course I had signed up for in my senior year, figuring it would give me an easy last quarter. I needed it to graduate. I hadn't taken one more unit than the absolute minimum required. After the final exam, the word got out that there had been a conspiracy. Seven of us were given Fs on the test, which meant in my case that I wouldn't be lining up for the June commencement. (The next spring I came back and retook the course and finally graduated, a year late.)

This all reached its absurd climax when the Student Judicial Council tried our case. It turned out that there wasn't much evidence to support the charge. Very few of the answers on our exams matched up. If we were conspiring to cheat in this course, we did a hell of a job of covering our tracks.

I was the last one scheduled for a hearing, and I admit I was pissed off by the time I walked into the room. My inquisitors were nine fellow students, waiting for me at a long polished table. The first question came from a guy I knew all too well. The previous year I had sat next to him in a history class, and that time I *had* cheated, that is, he and I had managed to discuss a few answers during one of the exams. Now here he sat self-righteously wanting to know whether or not I had fudged on the movie appreciation final. I thought, "Well, ain't you a beauty."

Out loud I said, "You goddamn hypocrite! From you I'm getting a question like *that?*"

It was all I needed to kiss the whole thing goodby. I told them I wasn't going to answer any of their Mickey Mouse questions. "I'm getting married," I said. "I'm leaving today. You people can do whatever you want to about it."

My fellow conspirators were eventually acquitted. But since I walked out on the hearings, the campus had no alternative but to give me an F and unceremoniously kick me out of the school, and out of that world. It was all fine with me. As far as I was concerned, college had served its purpose. I had already been welcomed, just as unceremoniously, into another world.

Just a few days earlier I had signed my first pro contract, in a brief meeting that confirmed all my vague impressions about the nature of professional ball. Sue was with me that time too. We drove up to San Francisco

26

together, and I left her behind the wheel, double-parked on Market Street, while I jogged up one flight of stairs to Tony Morabito's office.

This was before the days of six-figure contracts. Pro football was a different world than it is today. The players were basically the same as they are now coming out of college. But the world we entered was much different, much less in the public eye, much looser. At least that was true around 49er headquarters. Twelve years later I would be signing papers in front of TV cameras in the Jack Tar Hotel. In 1957 on the day of my first official contact with my new employers, Tony Morabito just stood up and walked out from behind his desk and shook hands and asked me how much I wanted.

I said I was thinking of something around $20,000. He was a small, friendly, intense man who enjoyed his role as father and friend to his ballplayers. He smiled regretfully, shook his head, and said that sounded a little high, that was pretty close to what the stars were getting, guys like Hugh McElhenny, and Y. A. Tittle. Since I was an untried rookie he was thinking of something closer to fourteen. He wasn't going to get tough about it though. He laid the contract on his desk and said I should fill in whatever figure seemed fair to me. "Take some and leave some." Then he left the room.

I calculated for about one minute, decided to split the difference between fourteen and twenty — to take about 40 percent, and leave about 60. I wrote in $16,000. Tony came back, looked it over, said that sounded all right to him. I told him I needed a little right now, and he said, "Take what you need out of your salary." So I mentioned a figure, and he wrote me out a check for $3000 right

27

there on the spot. I thanked him and jogged back down to the car. Sue and I drove immediately to a jewelry store, where we cashed the bonus check buying a ring.

The whole transaction in Tony's office had taken about ten minutes. This didn't surprise me at all, or strike me as anything unusual. It was exactly what I expected. The ease, the offhand manner — this confirmed my whole attitude toward pro football at that time; it was not anything anyone could take very seriously.

One thing to remember, this was before the days of bigtime television, which has made pro football an unavoidable presence in every American's life. My entire involvement had been with collegiate athletics. Up to that time I had only watched half-a-dozen professional games. My father took me to a couple when I was in high school. The others I viewed from the 49ers' sidelines. I had a friend at Stanford who worked in their equipment room in exchange for tickets, and he invited me along a few times so that my first exposure to professional ballplayers was picking up their jocks in the locker room and observing a behind-the-scenes manner that seemed to me much too blasé. They didn't seem to care very much about what they were about to go out and do. I had no idea then what was churning inside their stomachs while they joked around, suiting up.

In my eyes the average pro player was a slightly unsavory fellow cashing in on his abilities by making money to play a game he was obviously no longer committed to. It was strictly a business deal, devoid of emotional involvement. I told myself that I would certainly not be doing this for more than three or four years: make a little dough, get in and get out. In my mind the average pro was a chunky, somewhat bewildered guy from Chicago or Detroit who always seemed to be rising out of heavy mud. He had barely made it to the locker room from the bar closest to the stadium, and he and his cronies would be heading right back to the same bar after the game.

I remained ignorant until I was selected to play in the College All-Star Game at Soldiers Field in 1957. Pro ball was still so remote to me, I didn't even know who our opponent was until we got to Chicago. And whoever they were, I figured they didn't have a chance. We had such a great group of superior, dedicated, and emotionally involved college athletes, I didn't see how we could lose to these mudslingers from the East Coast.

Our opponents that day were the New York Giants, the team Jim Lee Howell had coached to the NFL championship. They had Charlie Conerly at quarterback, Frank Gifford, the all-purpose back who had won the Jim Thorpe Trophy the previous year, Andy Robustelli in the defensive line (and although it was not significant until eleven years later, one of the men defending against my passes was cornerback Dick Nolan, who came to San Francisco as head coach in 1968). During the first series I called after we got the ball, we ran five option plays, and the last one took us into the end zone. This was just the kind of thing I had expected. I was feeling pretty pleased, when Bill Svoboda, the Giants defensive captain and All-Pro linebacker, came up to me and said very softly, almost gently, "John, don't do that anymore. You're going to get killed."

I had never heard anything like this on a football field. The only kind of message I'd ever received from the opposition during a game was something on the order of,

"Okay, you sonofabitch. Your ass is grass and I'm a lawn-mower."

I must have looked surprised. Bill took the trouble to explain. "We really don't want to have to be defensing for that play. It puts a lot of pressure on us, and if you keep running it we are going to have to put a little pressure on you."

I was not going to be bullied by idle threats. When we got the ball back I called another option. Svoboda's move would decide the play. If he moved over to take care of the halfback drifting to the outside, then I would hold on to the ball and take it myself off tackle; if Bill moved on me, as I stepped down the line, I would pitch it out. Well, as soon as I took a step in his direction, Svoboda came for me. I pitched it, figuring he would then do what he was supposed to do and go after the halfback. He didn't. He couldn't care less about pursuing the play. He paid absolutely no attention to anything but me. He just kept coming. And BAM! The lights went out. I don't know what he did because I didn't see him. But when the lights came back on, I knew I had never been hit like that by anyone.

It was the first of many jolts that rainy afternoon. Very quickly I was educated toward a new definition of an important word I had long misunderstood. *Professional* meant a lot more than getting paid for your services. These guys were not just going through the motions. No one could play the game this well or know it this thoroughly unless he still cared a great deal about it. What's more, they beat us, 22-10.

Svoboda's tackle was a good lesson in respectfulness. But I still had a lot to learn. There was one pro ballplayer

30

in particular I did not respect, or wouldn't let myself respect. It was this fellow Tony Morabito had mentioned, the one whose job I would be competing for the next fall. Yelberton Abraham Tittle. I had seen him play once or twice in San Francisco and had not been too impressed. I was riding high. I really didn't see how this Tittle fellow could hold a candle to me. I knew he was famous. But, Jesus Christ, the man was already thirty, which seemed ancient to me then, and what was more to be pitied, the poor old guy was bald as an onion.

All Quarterbacks
Were Rivals

3 IN THEORY it's possible to have two starting quarterbacks who take turns running an offensive team. The Los Angeles Rams tried it for a while in the early fifties when they were looking for a way to keep Bob Waterfield and Norm Van Brocklin on the same ball club. It didn't work for long, though, because in practice such a setup is doomed, out of the question. Quarterbacks themselves can't tolerate this. It's enough trouble to be continually struggling with the coaches for control of what's happening on the field. To have another man always warming up on the sidelines, waiting for your knee to pop or your heart to fail — this is something a quarterback never gets used to. In his eyes the offensive team only needs one man in charge, and there's never much doubt in his mind who that should be.

Now, as of 1957, my rookie year, the 49ers had only known two starting quarterbacks. Frank Albert, the fiery little left-hander who had so much to do with making the T formation famous, played from 1946 through 1952. Y. A. Tittle unseated Albert in 1953 and he was still with

32

the team. He had watched half-a-dozen younger quarter-backs come and go. As far as he was concerned I was going to be another on that list. As far as I was concerned he was dead wrong about that.

That first season there was one other quarterback with the team. Earl Morrall, the All-American from Michigan State, had been the 49ers first draft choice the previous year. One night at training camp we were in a meeting for all the offensive backs and receivers when I said to Earl, "With this many quarterbacks, looks like one of us ain't gonna do much playing."

Morrall, who had spent most of the '56 season on the sidelines, leaned over to me and said, "Hey, John. If you think either one of us is going to play any football here, you'd better take another think, because the best quarter-back in the league is right here in this room."

He meant Tittle, of course. I just held on to that bit of advice. I didn't quite agree with it. Not then. Not until the season got well under way and I had the chance to watch Tittle closely for several games.

Meanwhile I had to suffer the indignity of having my own wings clipped a little. During an exhibition game against Cleveland, Frank Albert, who had become head coach, sent me in for my first series of plays, right after Joe Arenas, our halfback, ran a punt back fifty-two yards, all the way to Cleveland's six-inch line. When I went in we had a first down and goal to go. It didn't look like too much could go wrong, except that when I started my ca-dence, my voice cracked. Instead of the deep-throated HUT I was hoping for, it came out a high pitched *hoot*, as if someone had just squeezed my nuts. The center, Frank Morze, was so convulsed with laughter that the football came up wobbly, and I fumbled it. By this time the rest of our guys were laughing too hard to go looking for a fumble, so Cleveland recovered. As we came off the field, big Bob St. Clair, the team captain, went over to Albert and said, "Hey, tell your newfound protégé here to go out and buy himself a set of balls and come back and join us."

That was my opening shot at my new job. During the course of the first half I managed to fumble three more times, complete one pass, and throw the next one for an interception. Three minutes before the second quarter ended, Albert rescued me — or rescued the team — by putting Tittle back in. I found out many years later that when he got home that night, Y.A. and his wife opened a bottle of expensive wine in a little private celebration of my debut.

For the next ten games I sat on the sidelines, manning the phones to the spotters' booth and watching Tittle carefully, at first out of sheer competitive instinct, but gradually with more and more respect, and finally with outright admiration. He was doing things on the field I had never seen before. I had never seen them, partly because I had not been aware, until then, how much I didn't know, but mainly because Y.A., in his ninth pro season, was clearly a master of the art. He had accomplished what masters in any field accomplish. That is, he was making something difficult look simple. He had discovered for himself some basic principles of handling a football team, and he had broken them down into working fundamentals that gave his game a deceptive ease and smoothness.

At first I thought that much of what he did was due to

34

luck, when actually it was due to what he could *make* happen out on the field. Before a game he prepared himself so that he could take advantage of any pattern or weakness that might show in the other team. He would come into a game with his head full of ifs and buts and options for every situation. Once the game began, he was like a bridge player, keeping in mind everything happening on the field. He also knew what he himself could do best, and what his players could do best, and he would look for ways to apply these abilities to specific situations, because he also knew *when* a play would work best. By planning several moves ahead, he could set up a situation that would exploit a talent, or the surprise effect of a seldom used play.

The only way I could have absorbed this kind of wisdom, as a rookie with the 49ers, was by studying Tittle. The theory behind the team's offensive structure was not developed fully enough to account for it. These were skills Y.A. had worked out for himself, on his own. I did not fully appreciate then how hard won they were, how much experience lay behind them. But I did recognize a level of play unknown to me before. Just as the UCLA game had opened my eyes to what football was all about, observing Tittle throughout the '57 season really opened my eyes to quarterbacking as something a good deal more complex than passing the ball, and committing the playbook to memory, and waiting until kick-off to begin getting involved in the game.

I owed a lot to Tittle, and still do. But I didn't see it that way then, nor did I yet know how much more the game can mean as a man grows older. I was twenty-two and too much into my own trip to ever see the world from

Y.A.'s point of view. I only knew that I had been hired to play quarterback, and one way or another that's what I planned to do.

Earl Morrall was traded to Pittsburgh before the regular season started. That left the two of us. I figured it was just a matter of time. Y.A. was performing so well that first year, I didn't get onto the field until the second to last game, and then only for sixty seconds. But as things turned out, those sixty seconds were crucial to my future, and Y.A.'s too.

It was a game against the Baltimore Colts. If we won, we'd be tied for first place, with one game to play and our best shot at the conference title since the 49ers joined the NFL. Going into the fourth quarter we were behind 13-10, and things didn't look too bright. Y.A. was playing with a lot of pain. He had pulled a groin muscle in the Giants game the previous week. The Colts had been rushing him brutally all day. With a minute and a half left, he tried a second-down pass into the end zone. It fell incomplete. The line swarmed all over him. After the play he was writhing around on the grass and couldn't get up. Two guys had to help him off the field. I watched them staggering and hobbling toward the bench, and for a moment I was a spectator. My mind was up there in the stands somewhere, thinking what most of the fans must have been thinking, "What the hell do we do now?"

Albert called out, "Brodie!"

I didn't want to answer. This situation did not look at all like the rookie's big break. I wanted to push Y.A. back out onto the field, bum leg and all.

It was third down on Baltimore's fourteen. I joined the huddle and glanced around at the other players, all veterans, their faces running with sweat, their eyes aimed at me — veterans of this whole long game, and of the nearly finished season, veterans of many seasons with the team, guys like Bob St. Clair, Hugh McElhenny, Joe Perry, Clyde Conner, and Billy "Goose" Wilson, our tall, rangy, Everybody's-All-Pro end. What could I say to these guys that they didn't already know? All season I had been itching to play. Now it just seemed like a ridiculous time for me to be running into the game, with barely a minute on the clock and a conference title at stake. I was almost ready to laugh.

"Anybody got anything?" I asked.

Billy Wilson, in his firm, soft-spoken way, said, "Kid, just throw me a turn. Try to keep it low, and I'll get it."

I was glad for any suggestion. Most of the numbers were scrambling in my mind. My first thought at this point was getting out of the huddle in twenty-five seconds and getting a tight grip on the ball from center so I wouldn't lose it the way I had in that exhibition three months earlier.

This time I held on to it. I dropped back. The only thought in my mind now was, *Find Goose.* He had galloped down there into a perfect position inside the end zone. My pass was almost on target, but not as low as he wanted it. Just before it reached him, the defensive back popped him a lick in the back of the head, which knocked him, and the ball, and — in the estimation of a lot of the spectators — all our chances right out the window.

When we rehuddled we were still on the fourteen, with one down left and forty-seven seconds to play in the game.

Looking around at my elders I said, "What the hell do we do now?"

Hugh McElhenny, who had been switched from half-

37

back to end, said, "Throw the goddamn thing into the left-hand corner of the end zone. I'll be there. I can get around Milt Davis. Just keep everybody else out of the way."

Davis was a great cornerback. He had already intercepted one pass that day and run it back seventy-five yards for a touchdown. But McElhenny was a great receiver and one of the craftiest runners in football. I called the play. I dropped back again. The Colts' linemen were enthusiastic to say the least, rushing me so hard it was a toss-up who would make it to the pocket first — me or them. I looked for Mac in the end zone, and he was right where he said he'd be, and he had a step on Davis. I never did see him catch the ball. As soon as I let it go, I was hit by Art Donovan, the Colts enormous tackle.

The crowd went crazy, roaring and screaming, and for a moment I wasn't sure why. I was flat on my back, staring up at the sky, with Donovan on top of me.

I said, "What happened? Was it complete?"

Donovan grumbled something like, "How the hell should I know?"

Then the other guys came loping back, whooping it up, laughing and punching me and one another. We kicked the extra point, and after that there was only time for one more play from scrimmage. We beat them, 17-13.

Tittle was the happiest guy in San Francisco, hugging me and kissing me. A locker room picture came out on the *Chronicle* sports page showing him running his fingers through my sweaty hair. It was a great day for both of us. I had lucked out in my first regular-season appearance. He had led this team through the whole schedule and through fifty-nine minutes of the Colts game. At that

38

point, those sixty seconds didn't look like anything more than a rookie coming in to give the first-string guy a hand.

When I started the game against Green Bay the following weekend it was only because Tittle's leg still hurt him so bad. We had them 10-0 after one quarter, but Bart Starr was having a good day and doubled the score on us, putting Green Bay ahead 20-10 at the half. Tittle came off the bench to play the whole second half, a gimpy-legged hero, and pulled the game out of the fire, leading the team to a 27-20 win and a tie for the conference title.

Although we lost the play-off game to Detroit and thus a shot at the championship, this was the 49ers' best season up to that time. For Tittle, too, it was his best season so far. He played brilliant football all year long and won the Jim Thorpe Award as the players' choice for top performer in the league. You'd think his position would have been pretty secure. But a strange thing started to happen, something I later learned is not at all unusual in a quarterback's life. After that one pass to McElhenny, which I threw from the seat of my pants, my star started rising around 49er headquarters, while Tittle's unaccountably began to decline. It was nothing very noticeable at first, just a feeling. People began to refer to me as a winner. "The kid's a winner," they would say. Then Tittle's name came up and you'd hear something like, "Well, Y's a hell of a quarterback, nobody can deny *that*. But the leg is still giving him trouble, ya know. And hell, the guy *is* almost thirty-one."

By August of 1958 it was more than a feeling. At the end of training camp we always had a big intrasquad scrimmage, the first public exposure of the team before the exhibition season started. About five thousand spectators rimmed the field at St. Mary's College in Moraga, where we held our training camps. Before the game, the names of the starting players were announced, and they all jogged out onto the field to take the applause. Y.A. was announced as quarterback. Then the coaches called them back to the bench, and Red Hickey, the offensive backfield coach, delivered a ten-minute speech on the game plan to backs and receivers. When he finally said, "Okay, let's get started," Y.A. picked up a football, and he and I threw it back and forth a few times while Y worked his shoulder.

Red said to him, "What's the matter, Tittle? Aren't you warm?"

Y.A. said, "Hell no, I'm not warm. We been sittin' down for ten minutes."

Hickey turned to me. "Brodie, you warm?"

I wasn't any warmer than Tittle was. But I was looking for any opening at all. I said, "Yes, SIR! I'm always warm!"

"Okay, Brodie. You start the game."

Y.A. had two ways of getting angry. On the field he could just build up a fast head of steam and explode. I had seen him bellow at referees, rip his helmet off and hurl it at the grass. Off the field he was more likely to smolder. He would turn pink and seethe. This was his reaction when Red Hickey let me start the squad scrimmage in 1958. Y.A. didn't say a word. He glared. He clenched his jaws. He boiled, and he burned, and sat there on the bench, a Texas teakettle with the lid welded shut.

The scrimmage went well enough that it forced out into the open a competition which had not really existed beforehand. The coaches and a number of the players began to see it this way, and it was decided that Tittle and I would take turns playing half of each exhibition game to determine who should start the season. For me it was a great opportunity. For Tittle it was another goad, because this was not a fair way to judge the differences in our abilities.

Although a lot of people seem to overlook this fact, the purpose of exhibition games is to get the team ready for the season, a time of polishing and trying things out. Most veterans see it this way. They play hard, but because the games don't have the pressure or that sense of purpose you feel in a regular-season match, a guy like Tittle would not be exposing the full extent of his experience, whereas a young quarterback can come into an exhibition game and look like a star, because conditions are simpler. The other team will seldom run more than one or two basic defenses that they're trying to polish for the coming season. They won't try complex strategies or try to beat your best punch. They are concentrating on getting their assignments down. A young kid with some talent can go into an exhibition and look every bit as good as a guy who has been playing ten or twelve years. To Joe Fan — and sometimes even to a coach who has not himself played quarterback — the youngster will look great. And then he can fall on his fanny once the season begins, because a whole hell of a lot more starts happening on the field. The exhibition games test his potential but not his total experience or his ability to perform when every move and every decision counts.

Well, I wasn't too worried about all this. Playing half a game was better than playing no game at all. I was out

41

there throwing the ball at last. What I didn't know, or wouldn't let myself know, was the effect this began to have on Tittle. I wanted to play. He *had* to play. Yet here he was, ten years into pro ball, Most Valuable Player in the NFL, forced into a competition with a one-year veteran, for his team, and ultimately for his job.

He was insulted. He felt wronged. Once the regular season started, I was actually putting in more game time than Tittle was. It began to eat at his insides so bad, the times he did get into a game he couldn't hit a bull in the ass with a banjo. He'd do things he never would have done the year before. In one game against the New York Giants, Red Hickey told him not to throw the ball down the middle. "Don't throw a pass to the inside deep against the Giants," Hickey told him. In his inimitable way he added, "That little prick'll pick off everything you send there."

It wasn't bad advice. He was talking about Jimmy Patton, the Giants All-Pro safety, a small man for pro ball — 5-11, 170 pounds — but one of the quickest and the smartest. Yet from a quarterback's point of view I can understand why Y.A. disobeyed the order. If you go through an entire game and all you're throwing is short outs and hitches, you can start to get bored out there. You want a little variety in your calls. When your team is losing anyway, you get to a point where you want to try something different. I also feel that secretly Y.A. wanted to throw it down the middle just to prove Red was wrong and that he could beat Jimmy Patton for a touchdown.

Finally they were in a huddle and he said to Clyde Conner, our best receiver, "Hey, Clyde, can you beat Patton down the middle?"

Clyde said, "How the hell do I know? I haven't seen him all day. All I've been running is five steps and out."

Y.A. went ahead and called the play, threw it to Clyde who had cut inside and deep, and sure enough, Jimmy Patton intercepted it. He not only intercepted it, he ran it back eighty-five yards for a score.

On his way to the end zone, Patton scampered right toward Tittle. Y.A. seemed about ready to tackle him, but he didn't. He ran past Jimmy, on out into what had been the defensive secondary. I couldn't figure out what he was up to, and it remained a puzzle until we saw the game films a few days later.

The whole team was in the film room. When we came to that play, Hickey stopped the film. He rewound it and ran the play again, and we watched Y.A. run right past Patton, who was heading for the end zone. Without saying anything Hickey rewound the film and ran the play once more, and by this time everyone was covertly laughing at the spectacle of Y.A. ignoring Patton. We couldn't laugh out loud; it would have irritated Red. I was biting my lip, trying to hold it in. The room was filling up with snorts and snickers while Hickey ran the play three more times, then finally moved past it saying, "Well, god*damn.* I guess I never *will* understand this play."

I had no idea how humiliating that moment must have been for Tittle, not only the moment in the film room, with the whole team holding back its laughter, but that moment on the field. It turned out that he was running over to where Clyde had stopped and had pleaded with him, "Clyde, goddamn it, *please* tell Red that was your idea!"

That's how anxious and desperate he was. No man can

do anything when he's in that frame of mind. And as a quarterback, in charge of making as many decisions as that position demands, he didn't have a chance.

Years later Y.A. told me that after some games he would go home and sit on his bed and stare at the wall for hours, unable to speak, simmering with resentment and with self-disgust for the way he allowed himself to react, the way he let himself become the fool in this ridiculous situation. It was a kind of anger and anguish I had no comprehension of until nine more years went by, when the same thing started to happen to me. My time would come. I would reach the age Y.A. was then, with a Heisman Trophy winner just out of college and nipping at my butt, waiting for me to slip. My success would turn on me. But in 1958 I was young. I was cocky. I believed I was good enough to unseat Tittle, and the sooner the world found out about that the better. He was merely the man in front of me. As the feeling toward him started to change, I silently applauded, the same way he privately toasted my fumbles and interceptions. When the words of doubting about his abilities began to circulate, well, who could expect me to come to his defense. I was looking for any advantage that would allow me to play. All quarterbacks were rivals. Hadn't he done the same thing to Albert? Competition was the name of the game.

DIPLOMACY

DURING THOSE first two or three years, after I finally started doing some playing, a coach might come up to me with an idea I didn't much like and say, "I think this would be a good play to try in such and such a situation." And I would be likely to respond, "Oh shit, we can't do *that!*" I would hold him responsible for a bad idea rather than looking it over and saying, "Well, that *might* be a good thought, but the reason it can't quite work is that you're doing this, and what we could do is we could take your play and change it here, here, and here, and we might have something that works." Then I had an ally rather than an enemy on my own team.

It's really pretty simple. In order to get along with someone, you begin by discussing those things you agree on. You have to find some foundation of agreement. After that, you can agree to disagree. Even though I could see as clearly then as I do now how the play would work on the ball field, the way I handled the conversation is what had to change, and eventually did change. I just didn't understand yet how important it was for him to be on my side. I wanted to be the guy who made all the decisions, and I wanted to make sure everyone knew it. If we did okay, it was to my credit. Of course, if we didn't do okay, then the coach had blown it. That was a very juvenile attitude — the attitude of a guy who takes a low level of responsibility for his actions.

Albert's 49ers

4 TITTLE AND I may have been rivals. But we weren't enemies. We couldn't be, playing for the San Francisco 49ers in the late 1950s. Whatever struggle might have been developing between us happened inside the larger network of a team that was, at least for a while there, held together by a special spirit and sense of loyalty.

Being from the West Coast had something to do with this. We were sort of isolated out here, prone to stick together. At that time there were only two pro teams west of Chicago — the Rams in Los Angeles and us. Compared to most of the eastern teams, the 49ers had entered big league football late, in 1946, like a brash upstart from some uncharted part of the country. From the beginning it had been a loose, wide-open team. Win or lose, they played colorful football.

If any man epitomized the style and personality up to that time, it was Frank Albert, who had been associated with the 49ers since they pioneered the territory and was, for three lively years, head coach.

Ever since his spectacular career at Stanford, when he led the so-called "Cinderella Team" to the Rose Bowl in 1941, Albert had a reputation for a daring, unpredictable, spontaneous brand of football. He would pass when he was supposed to run; he would run when he was supposed to punt. Frank had to be daring and unpredictable. He was one of the smallest men ever to play the game professionally — 5-8, 160 pounds. When he took over the coaching job in 1956, the year before I got there, he was thirty-six years old, which made him the youngest head coach in pro ball at that time. He looked about ten years younger. They called him "The Boy Wonder." He hadn't changed much. He coached the same way he had played, and this gave the whole team a kind of freewheeling vitality both on and off the field.

Keep the pot stirring, that was Frank's specialty. Here's the kind of thing he would pull out of his hat — or maybe I should say, pull out of the seat of his chair. Frank had this little golfer's portable chair he carried around with him everywhere he went, the kind you can unfold and stick into the ground. In one game against the Philadelphia Eagles in 1958, Albie had his chair plugged in right next to the sideline stripe, and he sat there heckling Norm Van Brocklin all through the game. Everybody on our team got a kick out of this spectacle. Just as Norm reached the line of scrimmage, Frank would yell out something like, "Hey, Dutch, look out now, make sure you don't get any grass on that nice clean ass of yours."

After three quarters of this Van Brocklin finally got fed up. He was hunched down behind the center getting ready to call a play when Albert called him a chicken shit and a yellow-bellied sonofabitch, and Van Brocklin stopped the play. He stopped the whole ball game and stood up and turned toward Albert, who was sitting there rocking a little on his golfer's chair and flashing his shiny teeth out onto the field, and Norm shouted, "Albert, you weren't worth a shit as a player. Your players tell me nowadays you aren't worth a shit as a coach. Now will you shut the fuck up and let us get on with the game!"

Norm hunched over to call the play, then he stood up again.

"And another thing! Take that goddamn golf seat and stick it where it belongs!"

Our whole team fell apart laughing. So did Frank. He leaned back chortling with delight. He had rattled the Dutchman. This was the kind of thing he loved.

Although Frank was a hang-loose coach, he was also very nervous. In 1957 we were going into the Chicago game with six wins and one loss. He couldn't sleep the night before the game, so he took a sleeping pill, which didn't have any effect on him until six or seven in the morning. He dozed for a couple of hours and then fell asleep at the pregame meal. We roused him to get him to the stadium, and he took another pill to counteract the first one. We were in the locker room when he walked up to me and said, "Brodie, you get in there today, and don't fuck it up. All right?"

I said, "Frank, what are you talking about? I haven't played a series yet this year."

He said, "I know that. But if you *do* get in there, you're going to fuck it up."

That was for openers. After the game got started, I was standing by the bench, manning the phone. This was my first-year assignment, relaying messages from upstairs to the coaches and backs, or sometimes just handing them the receiver. Frank never liked the phones much. His tastes went back to the thirties, and all this equipment on the field was a little too technological for him. But every once in a while he'd come over and take a message. Late in the first half, there came a call for Frank. He grumbled and picked up the receiver just as J. C. Caroline, the Chicago defensive back, scooped up one of our fumbles and ran for a touchdown.

Frank said, "Oh shit," and threw the phone. I had crouched forward to watch this play, and the phone bopped me right square on top of the head. I didn't know what hit me. It damn near knocked me out. Gene Babb, a rookie fullback and my roommate that season, came off the field just then and saw me sitting on the bench in a daze, trying to clear my eyes and get my balance back. He said, "What the hell happened to *you*?"

"Albie just hit me on the head with the telephone."

Pointing his own battered head toward a pileup at the line of scrimmage he said, "Jesus, I thought *that* was tough. But it's pretty active right here!"

Midway through the fourth quarter of that same game, our line coach, Bill Johnson, was getting a little overheated. The game was very close, 17-14, with Chicago ahead, but we were driving hard. We were on their thirty-five-yard line, when the referee called a five-yard penalty on us. Bill was so agitated he jumped out onto the field, six or seven yards past the sideline stripe. The ref came over and said, "Albert, you keep this man off the field or I'm going to penalize you another fifteen yards."

Frank said, "What are you talking about?"

The ref said, "Who is this guy anyway?"

Frank said, "Hell, I don't know. I never saw him before in my life."

50

So the ref called the police to come down and get Bill off the field — Bill Johnson, who had played center with the team since 1948 and had been offensive line coach for the past two years. They walked him right out of the ball park and he had to imagine the end of that game by interpreting the crowd noises that reached him in the parking lot. He didn't speak to Albert for about three months.

But the funniest thing is, we won that ball game, shenanigans and all. That was the atmosphere the year the 49ers tied for their first conference title. Crazy as he was, Frank enjoyed the hell out of football, and he helped everybody else enjoy it too.

I learned a lot playing on Frank's teams. He helped me keep in mind that no matter how much seemed to be at stake, never to forget it was a game. And he had his priorities in order. The smartest ballplayer in the world can become a coach, but unless he has an affinity with the men who are still playing, he will get into deep trouble. Sooner or later his hole card will get checked. When the going gets rough, when the stress time comes, the players don't care if the coach seems like a nice guy and can speak very eloquently; there is always a moment of truth, in the heat of the game, where the players find out if a man is for real. Is he interested in getting the team going in the right direction? Or is he interested in proving that he is right and someone else is wrong? No matter how smart you are, if you don't have this affinity with your group, eventually you'll lose them. They'll see that you have overlooked something essential to the playing of the game. And Frank, as a coach, was never that way; he was always with his ballplayers.

After a game, for instance, if a reporter came back to the

locker room looking for a story and said to Frank, "Ya know, it's too bad Y. A. missed on two or three of those plays; it looked like he had the man wide open and he just missed it," Frank's first reaction would not be, "Well, that's true, but those things do happen." He would never take that kind of bait. He would be more likely to say, "Well, you sonofabitch! A guy makes twenty-five good throws and all of a sudden he throws one or two bad ones, and you figure that's the reason we lost the game? Shee-it! Listen! Anything that Tittle did in this game tonight is the reason we came as close as we did!"

This supportive attitude created the kind of allegiance that can make a team move. And it helped to hold us all together.

On road trips, as soon as we got into town, there would be a meeting in the lobby of the hotel. Nobody would be breaking off into little cliques of two and three, with guys muttering, "Hey, I'll see you at so-and-so's." There were thirty-three guys on the team, and someone would announce, "All you guys who are going out, we'll meet back here in the lobby in fifteen minutes."

We drank together, went out to dinner together, raised hell together. One Thanksgiving weekend we were in Washington, D.C., to play the Baltimore Colts, and we all went out to a kind of semiprivate burlesque house, where we got into a regular cowboy-movie brawl. The whole damn team. It was after curfew, which made it even wilder. We were feeling pretty cocky, and not trying very hard to be quiet. Somebody in our gang offered to buy a round of beers for everyone else in the room. At one of the other tables there were four local guys, also feeling salty, and maybe they were Colts or Redskins fans to boot, and they said something like, "We don't want any beer." One of our guys said, "What did he say?" The other guy stood up and repeated himself: "I said we don't want any of your goddamn beer!" Well, one thing led to another pretty quickly after that, and the whole place exploded, with tables and chairs flipping over and crashing, women screaming, and glasses flying through the air.

When it was over we cleaned the place up, and twenty-five of us snuck back into the hotel without getting caught.

Bob St. Clair had cooked up that expedition. He was team captain and also team ringleader. Frank Albert was one of the smallest men to ever play pro ball; St. Clair was one of the tallest: 6-9, 265 pounds. We called him "The Geek" because he ate raw meat. He'd go into a restaurant and order steak. The waiter would ask him how he wanted it and Bob would say, "Raw." The waiter would say, "You mean rare?" Bob would say, "I mean get the meat out of the freezer and thaw it a little and bring it out here to the table."

St. Clair was the kind of guy you had to respect. Not only for his size. But also for his generosity. He was a big man, in every sense of the word. Once a rookie made the team, St. Clair made sure he was included in whatever was happening. Billy Wilson and Y. A. Tittle were the same way. With them there was none of this veteran versus rookie separation. They knew how important it was for everyone to have that sense of working together for the common cause. As a young guy just entering the world of pro football, I couldn't have asked for a more congenial place to start.

Mister Clean

5 I GIVE TITTLE special credit. He left all his competitive resentments out there on the football field. It can make for a tense relationship when a man is both your teammate and your rival. But it was a point of honor with Y.A., once I made the team, to try and get along.

The feeling between us would show from time to time, of course, in muted ways. Particularly during the card games. There were about six guys on the 49ers who played bridge all the time, and Tittle and I were two of them. At the bridge table we would needle each other. More was involved, you see, than simply our competition as quarterbacks. Our styles and our origins were far apart. He came from east Texas, where he had been playing football at the age of ten, competing fiercely in those Texas leagues that begin in the sixth grade. He felt that football was the only thing he had ever been any good at. He had been fighting hard all his life, always reaching for something that seemed to be just beyond his grasp. Whatever he had achieved, he felt he owed it all to foot-

54

ball. And here I came, a Stanford kid, glib and cocky, and in his eyes not yet nearly serious enough about the game. He used to call me *Mister Clean.*

When we played bridge he would needle me about my careful and sometimes holier-than-thou approach to cards. He would do this partly because he himself had acquired the reputation for finagling and peeking at other hands; he needed a scapegoat of his own. These were our roles at the bridge table. I would be the clean-cut kid from the well-to-do western campus who never cheated at cards. Y.A. would be the man of the world who had come up the hard way and knew what it took to survive. You know how these things go. On the surface it was all friendly kidding. Below the surface we were pushing each other's buttons. One week Y.A. got a bit tired of being the bad guy all the time. He figured he didn't finagle any more than the next man and that I did not finagle any less. He set about to give this theory a test.

There were four of us who played just about every night — Y. A., Matt Hazeltine, Mike Dukes, and me. This particular night it was Mike and me versus YAT and Hazel. We were set up in the corner of what was known as the "corner room" of the Moraga training camp. Y.A. shuffled. Mike cut. While Y.A. dealt, nobody was saying much, none of the usual gags about how smug I looked or how shifty Tittle looked. I wasn't noticing this. I was concentrating on my cards. I ran the bid up to six spades. Then just as we finished the first play, the telephone rang.

Someone down the hall answered and yelled out that it was for Mike. He said he'd be right back, and he excused himself. As soon as Mike stepped out the door, Hazeltine pushed his chair back and said he had to go to the can so

55

he might as well go now. Then Y.A. got up and said he felt like getting himself a bottle of beer.

There I sat, studying my hand, and waiting for my buddies who had all left theirs fanned out on the table. I did not know then that Y.A. and Hazel had spent four hours that afternoon rigging the deck to create this spread of cards I was looking at. I did not know that Y.A. had dragged in a fourth accomplice to answer the phony phone call from a fifth accomplice. Nor did I know that they had purposely set up the table so that my back would now be to the window. I only knew that I had bid six spades, that I could make four with ease, that making six was going to be a bitch, but a real coup if I could bring it off. As they left the room I had been thinking, "Jesus, I'd love to get this one. It would stick it right in his ear." It would devastate Y.A., who hated to lose and hated worse to get skunked. To do it, I had to make four or five very sharp decisions, and that of course would be a whole lot easier if I had just a little hint of what was in his hand.

I began to get restless. I shifted my weight. I closed my cards together, and fanned them out again, and looked at the backs of the cards face down on the table in front of Y.A.'s empty chair and Matt's empty chair. Where the hell did everybody go? I listened. It was quiet, just Mike down the hall muttering into the telephone. I thought to myself, "That sonofabitch Tittle cheats at everything and doesn't think anybody in the world knows what he's up to. Hell, I'll just give him some of his own medicine."

I put my cards down carefully, leaned forward and reached across the table with both arms, quickly slid a thumb under Tittle's hand and Matt's hand, scanned all the faces, replaced the cards, and sat back.

56

He waited a beat. Then I heard his slow Texas drawl, right behind me.

"O ho *ho.*"

I turned around. The window was open. He was leaning on the sill triumphantly, with a grin as wide as the part in his hair.

"Well now, Mister Clean, what have we here?"

GAMBLING MEN

WE NEVER had much money riding on those games. A quarter of a cent a point. Winner might walk away six dollars and thirty-one cents richer at the end of a long night. But we always had something riding on the game. Just to salt it. We would never play for nothing. At the card table there always had to be a little something at stake. Different games, you might have a good deal more at stake. Because I have met very few quarterbacks who don't like to have something riding on whatever game it is they're playing — except the big one, of course — the one they're paid to play on Sunday afternoon. I don't know many quarterbacks, for instance, who would play a round of golf just to be playing golf, or who would play for a quarter or for fifty cents a hole. Maybe the fifth time they play they'd like to play for twenty-five dollars, and you can take it on up from there.

They want to get some enthusiasm up for the playing — that is part of it. Like anybody else, they want the contest to have an edge. But in the case of quarterbacks, there is more to it; they gamble in a sort of special way.

58

And I am not talking about gambling illegally in order to make a killing on the outcome of a big football game. This is what terrifies the National Football League and keeps them sending out undercover agents to check up on quarterbacks. They'll hear that some guy is betting heavily at the races or on a golf match or is running around with professional card players, and they automatically assume that sooner or later he is going to be betting on his own team. Pretty soon the owner of the ball club is calling up asking about your associations and saying, "Hey, you better cut down on your bets." Well, what they have failed to perceive is the difference between gambling and "fixing," between illegal tactics, or wild and reckless behavior, and gambling as a way of life, a way of making life interesting.

A quarterback is by nature a certain kind of gambling man. I would go so far as to say that if a man does not like to gamble, he probably won't be a quarterback. There are exceptions to this, of course. But I have rarely met a professional quarterback who is not a hell of a gambler, of one kind or another. It is an aspect of gamesmanship that most quarterbacks like. It is as natural to them as releasing the ball, because a quarterback enjoys the action; he likes to be in that position of decision; he likes to take the responsibility for winning or losing; he likes to test his wits against another man's. On the ball field every play you call is a kind of gamble, a calculated risk. And yet you have to think that you have some kind of edge on the other guy, that, all other things being equal, you are going to be smart enough to win.

Taking Over

6 ON THE PRACTICE FIELD and during games, the tension between Tittle and me continued to mount, all through my first four years with the team. In 1958 I actually put in more game time than he did. In 1959 he started most of the games. In 1960 it was about a tossup. It got to be a very unhealthy situation. We were both using up a lot of effort fencing with each other — effort that should have been going into defeating other teams. And it has to be said that Red Hickey, who became head coach when Albert quit at the end of the 1958 season, did not do a lot to improve things.

Hickey, who had been a tough end at the University of Arkansas the same years Frank was at Stanford, and who had been a very effective assistant coach with both the L.A. Rams and the 49ers, was a different kind of man. He was more demanding, sterner on discipline, and prone to impulsive, inconsistent decisions — like the time he started me in the squad scrimmage in 1958. It came out of nowhere. After a couple of seasons of that sort of thing, Tittle and I both had the jitters, wondering where we stood.

60

Here's the kind of thing that would happen. In 1959 we flew to Wisconsin to play Green Bay, and right up to game time, we still did not know which one of us was going to start. This had become the pattern. Red wouldn't name a starter until after we had warmed up and trotted back to the locker room. We would do anything we could think of to influence him — smile, ask him how his wife was feeling, or try to be the last man to throw a complete pass before we left the field. If Red saw you throw a bad warm-up pass, that might be the image he took with him to the locker room when he was trying to make up his mind. So before the Green Bay game we stood out there going through the motions of warming up and pretending not to be noticing the other guy's performance. Yet we were acutely aware of each other and, I have to admit, slightly amused by this foolishness we'd been forced into.

Neither of us wanted to be seen throwing an incomplete. We would discourage our receivers from running long. I would pull my receivers in a little closer, and finally Y.A. would say, "Hey, Brodie, for Christ sake, why don't you throw the goddamn football." And he would pull his receivers in a little closer. I would say, "Jesus Christ, we could hold this workout in a phone booth." Then, as I continued to throw my eight-yard-jog-and-nothing passes, I would say, "Tittle, if you're not going to *throw* the goddamn thing, why don't you go on up in the stands and buy yourself a hot dog."

Before long the receivers were in so close we were both lobbing three- and four-yard passes and trying so hard not to laugh that neither one of us ever did get warm.

When we got back to the locker room, instead of using

61

that time the way we should have, to clear our minds and get completely focused on the game, we couldn't relax until Red made his decision. This time he happened to smile on me. "Okay, John, I'm going to go with you tonight." So I started, and in the first half I threw zero for thirteen, didn't connect on a single pass, not even an interception, and we didn't score a point. Green Bay was ahead of us 28-0 when Red put Tittle in. Y.A. got two touchdowns for us, but it wasn't enough. Green Bay went on to win it, 48-14 — a clear indication to me of how distorted this whole situation had become.

Although we had been able to find the humor in that warm-up routine, by the end of the 1960 season, nothing was funny anymore. Tittle was so pissed off he would hardly speak to me. He was so fed up with the way things were going, and so overwhelmed by it all, he was just about ready to get out of the sport completely. When he was traded to New York at the beginning of the '61 season, he resented it so much he almost didn't go. Luckily for him and for football, that trade turned out to be the best thing that ever happened to him. He said later it was like an anvil had been lifted from his shoulders. They loved him in New York. Fans back there organized whole rooting sections to yell out YAT, YAT, YAT.

There was a premonition of this new love in the way the Giants themselves behaved when we played them in Portland early in the '61 exhibition season. Each time they hit Tittle, they would pull their punches. Sam Huff hit him one time and was heard to mutter, "Don't get hurt, Y.A., don't get hurt." It was his first solid clue that a trade to the Giants was in the offing. The players in New York had heard about it before he had. He was like a little baby to them. The linemen would hit him, then hold on, so he wouldn't land too hard.

When his trade was completed, before the regular season opened, it did not mean I had seen the last of Y.A. We would be meeting again soon, as opponents, and later on in situations neither one of us could have foreseen in 1961.

Meanwhile I took over as undisputed quarterback for the 49ers, which made his trade seem like the best thing for both of us. We were both playing. He had a team. I had a team. In fact, Red Hickey had dreamed up an offense that was supposed to exploit my special assets as a "triple-threater." (Which was something else that agitated Tittle. He never could get the hang of this new system, and it really was the final step in his departure for the East.) It was called the "shotgun." For a while it made things look as if the 49ers were still the razzle-dazzle outfit we were reputed to be. The shotgun came with double-barreled action, and the press liked that. The name sounded right for a team called the "Forty-Niners." Hickey once said, "The shotgun is a thing that you can swing in any direction and fire when ready." For a while, for about half-a-dozen games, the damn thing actually worked.

It was nothing new. It was a little like the old double wing formation, with the quarterback taking the ball seven yards deep. The theory was that this gave him a passing or running choice on every play. Hickey had revived it because he thought professional offenses were becoming too stereotyped, and that defenses were too — which was true.

The shotgun had its advantages and disadvantages. I didn't like the running part of it much. I *could* run fairly well by that time, but it never made much sense to me to build plays around a running quarterback when we had running backs who could do it better. What bothered me more, though, was that it eliminated all the short passing routes because of the time it took to get the ball from center and get it gripped right. The ball came back, you caught it, you moved, you got the laces aligned, you had to glance down at the laces, and then you looked out at the field to see what was going on. With the T, as soon as the ball is snapped, it's ready for release.

The shotgun's main advantage was surprise. It was a gimmick more than anything else. Near the end of the 1960 season, Hickey had introduced it as a desperation measure for dealing with Baltimore. In that case it was a good move. Baltimore was a better team, and the only way we could have beaten them was to surprise the hell out of them. Which we did. By mixing shotgun plays with T formation plays, we won that game and two more. When the '61 season opened, with me in charge, we skunked two teams we weren't even supposed to come close to.

The surprise element had two varieties: the confusing and the ridiculous.

At one point Red introduced a series of plays that sent the quarterback plunging into the line from about six yards back. This was the height of the ridiculous part and what ultimately drove Y.A. into open defiance against him. Tittle just thought it was the craziest thing he'd ever been asked to do in a football game. It was a goal-line play, called Q-1, Q-2, etc. I can remember calling this

64

once in a game against the Rams. I called a Q-5, spun and faked to the halfback coming around, then drove into what was supposed to be a hole between Deacon Jones and Merlin Olsen, L.A.'s All-Pro defensive linemen and definitely the toughest tackle-end combination in football. Deacon weighed 260; Merlin weighed 270. I weighed about 195 that season. I was going to split those two guys apart.

I managed to pick up three yards on the play and almost broke both my ankles. Deacon Jones was worse off than I was. I thought they were going to have to carry him out of the game on a stretcher. He was so crippled with laughter he could barely get up. He said, "John, just what in the hell are you trying to *do?*"

He and Merlin were looking at me like I had lost my mind. I could hardly keep from laughing out loud myself. I said, "Shit, don't ask me. I'm just the fullback."

The amazing thing was the confusion that stunts like this created in the opposing defense. Our first season game in 1961 was against Detroit. We beat them, 49-0. They had one of the tightest defensive systems in the league, but against the 49ers none of their keys were working. The linebackers would see our guards going one way, and follow them, only to find the play heading in the opposite direction. Our two halfbacks would line up outside the offensive tackles and about one yard behind the line of scrimmage, which could put five receivers downfield right away, creating patterns that Detroit's secondary just wasn't programmed for.

It was actually a hell of a lot of fun. I'll never forget Joe Schimdt and Wayne Walker looking at each other after one play — and these were two of the smartest linebackers ever to play the game — and Schmidt said, "Jesus Christ, who had the ball?" Wayne said, "I don't know who had the ball. I don't even know what the hell these guys are doing!"

The same thing happened the next weekend when we met L.A. and tromped them, 35-0. Then we played the Vikings and beat them, 38-24. Any doubts I might have had about the shotgun were pretty dim in the face of three straight wins and 122 points. We were so hot, we figured we had pioneered a whole new wave of football strategy. That was precisely when the bubble burst. It took about that long for other teams in the league to decide they were going to have to get serious about whatever it was San Francisco was throwing at them. Clark Shaughnessy, defensive coach at Chicago in those days, got hold of the game films, took the formation apart, and did a brilliant job of mapping out a defense for it. After all, he had been watching football games for a long, long time. He'd been around when that formation first came out.

We went up against the Bears for the fourth game that season, and they whipped our ass, 31-0. It wasn't totally the offensive formation that failed us — we were overconfident, had a false sense of power — but that was the beginning of the end of the shotgun. When we lost the fifth game to Pittsburgh, a team we should have beaten, it was clear that everyone was seeing through its flaws. We went back to the blackboard.

The shotgun was more than a short-lived flash of offensive strategy. In my view it was symptomatic of something regrettable that was happening to the team. Between seasons Hickey had done some personnel shuffling to support the shotgun concept. He had drafted with that

66

in mind. He had traded with that in mind. For various reasons we had lost several key players, including Tittle, and Hugh McElhenny, and Billy Wilson. When the shotgun started to misfire, the team was in real trouble. We had to rethink our offense after the season was under way and switch around some assignments. This led to confusion and disagreement, and I found myself tangled up in a new and unfamiliar situation — new and unfamiliar because I was now *the* 49ers quarterback.

It was most evident in what I was hearing from the stands. Among the things I had inherited from Tittle — along with the ball — were the notorious boo-birds in Kezar Stadium. Their cries taught me an important lesson. A lesson in responsibility. Many fans tend to follow the ball on every play, assuming that wherever the ball goes, so goes the fate of the game. And since the quarterback in the T formation handles the ball on every play, these fans figure that when the play goes right, it is his achievement; when the play goes wrong, it is his fault. Thus when the team goes wrong, the quarterback is the man who should get booed. The San Francisco fans had booed Frank Albert. They had booed Y. A. Tittle. By the time I took over the team, it had become a local tradition, and the tumult would sometimes sound, from midfield, like waves of thunder rolling overhead. But until I took over the team I had not really had to deal with this in any sort of permanent way because I had not been the number-one guy.

San Francisco, I eventually learned, was a special case. Players from other teams would shake their heads in amazement at what passed between the fans and the field. At Kezar there's a tunnel leading from the locker rooms to the field. The tunnel opening cuts into the stands so that thirty feet of the ramp are lined with sloping walls where fans used to wait, sometimes hundreds of them, some cheering us on, waving programs, others hurling wadded-up paper cups, beer cans, or bottles of beer.

After one very close game against Baltimore, which they won, I went over to John Unitas to congratulate him and say hello. We started walking toward the tunnel together, and as we neared the ramp, I said, "John, you better put your helmet on."

He kind of smiled, as if to say I was overly nervous because I'd been getting booed a lot toward the end of the game.

I went ahead and put my helmet on and said, "Once you get near that group, it's a little active."

"It can't be that bad," he said.

We moved on into the tunnel and nothing much had happened, but I knew the worst part was yet to come. On the other end there was a fifteen-foot railing usually swarming with fans after a game, and all kinds of surprises could be waiting for you. I said, "Hey, John, I'm not kidding. Put on that helmet."

So he did, begrudgingly, and just a moment later a beer bottle someone had aimed at me whistled past my head and clanged against his ear.

"Jesus Christ," Unitas said, "they *mean* it!"

"You're damn right they mean it."

He didn't hear my last line. He was running for the locker room.

When he was still head coach, Frankie Albert once came into the locker room at half time with his sportcoat completely soaked in beer. Someone had just poured a

68

whole mugful of it over his head. "Sonofabitch," he cried gleefully, "they must think *I'm* out there playing."

By 1967 it got so bad the stadium officials built a wire cage with cyclone fencing over the exposed part of the ramp. That didn't stop some of the fans. They fell into the habit of dropping hot pennies through the mesh, aiming for the space between the back of the neck and the shoulder pads.

Like I said at the beginning, it's an education, playing quarterback. You have to learn to dodge hot pennies, duck flying beer cans, and when the booing starts, you have to figure out a way to keep your cool. You might say that in the long run, playing at Kezar was a great training ground. It could magnify any little weakness and really put you to the test. If I could apply my attention to a ball game in that arena in the early sixties, I could be free from distraction in any stadium in the country.

But it took a while to figure out why they were booing *me,* why I should bear the brunt of the team's performance, and a while longer to rise above this and not let it affect my game. That meant giving some thought to who, in this football club, was responsible for what. A quarterback is always caught in what you might call the zone of responsibility — and this is the kind of thing that creates a lot more tension than any number of monster-men rumbling toward him from the line of scrimmage. He will either learn to thrive on it or it will overwhelm him. From the fan's point of view he is the man most responsible for what is happening on the field. And he is. But there are also some areas not within his responsibility. If the pass is incomplete, it could be his ailing arm, or it could be the receiver's ailing legs, or it could be that the whole struc-

69

ture of the team's offense is badly put together. But when the game starts, however things stand, he has to go to work. Joe Fan doesn't much care what has gone on behind the scenes. Joe Fan knows that the quarterback is in charge, and if things are going wrong, he is the one you boo.

A lot of coaches share this outlook, especially when the team is losing. If the team is losing, the quarterback is out there screwing up again and not following orders. If the team is winning, it's because he has finally got the coach's instructions straight.

Now if you are mature and on top of things, you don't waste energy fighting this arrangement. Absorbing the brunt of this abuse from the stands is as much a part of the quarterback's job as pinpointing a sideline pass. You let the booers go ahead and boo, and you go play well enough to silence it. You let the coaches point their fingers and tear their hair, or do whatever the hell they're going to do, while you look for ways to live with it all, and not get vindictive, and keep on getting the job done — which for the quarterback includes *understanding* why things are working, or failing to work.

Eventually I learned what kind of offense worked best for me and how I could put this into motion. I learned what my responsibilities were in every conceivable situation: what could be solved by the coaches, by the players, by the offense, the defense, and how to talk about it when trouble started. But I was less experienced in 1961 and '62. I did not yet completely understand the routes my receivers could run best or the types of passes I threw best. Nor did I take into consideration the personalities of the men in our offensive line; this had not figured in the kinds of decisions I was allowed to make. Thus, after

At Stanford, 1956.

Suited up for the College All-Star game, 1957.

This was just before Albert hit me with the phones — my rookie year with the 49ers, 1957. (In background, at far left, Billy Wilson; at the table, Joe Perry; behind me in helmet, Hugh McElhenny.)

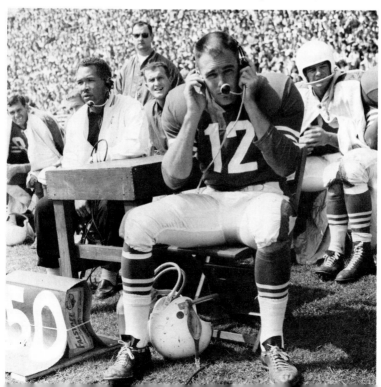

Albert's 49ers, 1958. I'm at the left end of the middle line, next to Tittle, No. 14, and behind Bob St. Clair, No. 79. Billy Wilson is behind me, No. 84. Four men from this team are now in the Football Hall of Fame: Tittle, Hugh McElhenny, No. 39 (far right); Leo Nomellini, No. 73 (far right); and Joe Perry, No. 34 (front, center).

Photo courtesy San Francisco 49ers

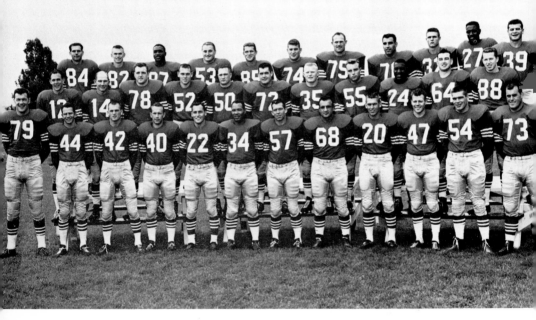

I am not trying to imitate a Russian dancer. I'm running the Shotgun against Minnesota, 1961.　Photo by Arthur Rickerby, for *Life*. © Time, Inc.

After we filed the Shotgun, we went back to the T. This is the 1962 Viking game at Kezar. I'm handing off to Billy Kilmer, who played halfback for a while.　Photo by and courtesy of Frank Rippon

With John David Crow and
Y. A. Tittle in 1965. I can't
repeat what we were talk-
ing about.

Photo by Ken Yimm, courtesy Palo
Alto *Times*

Here's Jack Christiansen
getting ready to hunker
down for a sideline con-
versation.

Photo by Fred Kaplan, for *Sports
Illustrated.* © Time, Inc.

A family reunion in Spokane, Washington, in 1967, with my brother, Bill, my sister, Katie, Dad, and Mom.

"Hiding out" at Punaluu, Hawaii, with Sue and the kids in 1966.

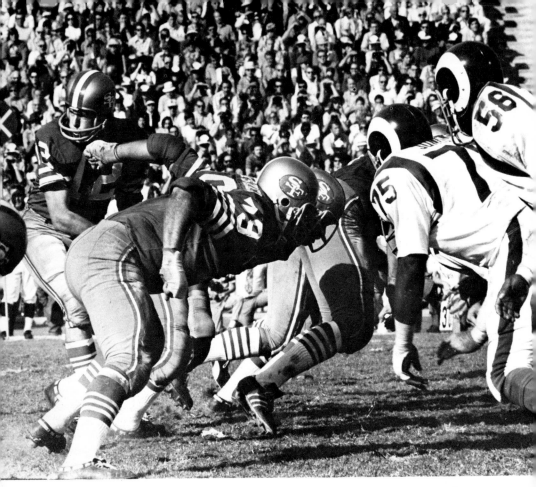

No. 75 is Deacon Jones of the L. A. Rams. Who says anybody gets tense out there?

Photo by and courtesy of Bill Nichols

This is what it looks like to a halfback. The guy peering over the top of No. 74 is Green Bay's linebacker, Ray Nitschke.

That's not a cigar coming through the face mask. It's my tongue.
Photo by and courtesy of Frank Rippon

Me and my buddies from the Rams front line, Deacon Jones, No. 75, and Merlin Olsen, No. 74. Gene Washington, No. 18, is in the foreground.
Photo by and courtesy of Frank Rippon

five years in pro ball, I still did not really have a personality of my own on the field — partly because I had not yet been given a chance to *take* responsibility for certain features of the offensive game and partly because I did not yet understand myself very well.

As long as Tittle was in front of me, I could concentrate on beating him out. Once I was playing, the struggle changed. I had to deal directly with the coaches, and the fans, and with myself. Which is not to say that it kept me from playing good football. Statistically 1961 was a very good year. I was rated fourth among all the passers in the NFL. In average yards gained, I led the league, with 9.14 yards per pass attempt. Nineteen sixty-two was, in many ways, a good year too. I had a lot of exhilarating days when nothing else mattered but the next pass, the next series of plays, the downfield drive to the end zone.

As one advantage of knowing that I was now the starting quarterback, I was free to do more during the course of a game. While competing for the job, a lot of my attention had been directed toward doing what the coaches wanted me to do, whether I thought it was productive or not, just so I could continue playing. I would avoid a chancy play for fear that a missed pass could take me out of the ball game. And there's something else that suffers in that kind of competitive situation: the communication between a quarterback and other backs and receivers. Now, for the first time, I was starting to get together with receivers on the practice field and really talk about what patterns each guy liked to run. This had a lot to do with our upset victory over Green Bay on one of the truly fine days during those first years I was in charge of the team.

The Packers were on their way to the 1961 champion-

ship. Their defense was legendary. It wasn't complicated; it was just thorough. Because they were so well
prepared and so on top of what offenses were doing, they
held to one basic formation and made adjustments inside
it. They had taken our offense apart and keyed on some
obvious features in our passing attack that we ourselves
had never noticed until the game began. Our backs and
ends usually ran complementary patterns. For instance,
any time our fullback went wide, they knew the flanker
back was going to be turning in, taking an inside break.
So one of their linebackers would drop right into the hole
our primary receiver was heading for. Green Bay was so
well coordinated the strongside linebacker would keep
his hole covered just long enough for the middle linebacker to get over there, then he would move out on the
fullback so that both receivers would be covered.

Well, when I saw this happening, I was able to respond
in a way I never would have in 1959 or '60. I thought to
myself, "Why in hell do we have to keep running it that
way?" Once I saw what they were keying on, it was just
a matter of taking away their keys. In the huddle we
began to work out counterroutes. Instead of sending the
flanker to the inside with the fullback wide, we sent him
to the outside, or on a hook-and-go. This surprised Green
Bay. They didn't expect us to have that much flexibility.
Our receivers, Bernie Casey, R. C. Owens, Monty Stickles, and Clyde Conner, would come back to the huddle
with bits and pieces of information about how a route
could be adjusted to take advantage of some adjustment
Green Bay had made.

We started mixing up these counterroutes with our normal routes. Pretty soon they didn't know what to expect.

72

They weren't ready for this. We were controlling the ball with pass patterns. R. C. Owens was a receiver who could really jump in a crowd and catch the ball. He didn't have a lot of speed, but he used what he had very deceptively. He caught about twelve passes that day. Bernie Casey, who was that other kind of receiver, a real speed burner, caught six, two of them for touchdowns.

Green Bay was leading 21-19, when we got the ball back on our own twenty-five, with two and a half minutes to play. By this time the Packers' defense didn't know what we were going to do. On the first play I called one of our counterroutes, a swing pass, with the flanker running to the outside. This got their cornerback playing deeper; he didn't want to overcommit himself either way now, and he wasn't too sure what his outside linebacker was going to do because that man wasn't playing it like their game plan said it should be played. Then I called one of those plays the Packers had been so well prepared for when the game began — the fullback swinging wide to the outside, with R. C. Owens turning to the inside. R.C. caught it. Figuring they would now be set up for a counterroute, I called the same play again, and R.C. caught it again. And since it had worked so well twice in a row, I called it again, a turn to the inside, and R.C. caught another one. Bam, bam, bam, bam — four quick passes that brought us down to their fifteen-yard line, where Tommy Davis came in to kick a field goal that won us the ball game, 22-21.

It was the only game the Packers lost all season. But that wasn't really what made it so sweet. Even if we had lost it, somehow we had the feeling that the game was "ours." There had been so much input from every guy on

73

the team throughout the game, we genuinely felt it belonged to us.

Games like that were almost enough in themselves to justify my existence. And yet, something was missing. It was not anything I could identify at the time. Nothing tangible. An empty space. It had to do with the gap between my life on the field and my life off the field, and the way I kept these two parts of my life almost entirely separate.

The ball field was like a big security blanket. It was the only world I really enjoyed and the only world I felt comfortable in. Leaving it was a little like going into a foreign country. All my achievement was happening out there in the public eye on Sunday afternoon. I gave a lot of myself, my effort, my ability; and I took a lot. Off the field it didn't work that way. I only took. I caroused and raised hell and went out drinking with the boys. At home I just loafed around. We had three kids then, but I wasn't spending much time with them. I was spending my time on things I thought a football player ought to be doing. I was trying to live up to the image of a professional football player. It wasn't an image I had created for myself. It was one I had picked up somewhere along the line. I was trying to be what I thought was important for a ballplayer to be. And of course there is no such animal. No group of people is more diverse than professional ballplayers. They come in all sizes and shapes and colors and from all parts of the country. Nothing could be more naive than the idea of a "typical" ballplayer.

But that is what was motivating me in those days. I was, in short, the total EFFECT of something far outside myself rather than CAUSE.

74

I didn't know this at the time. I only knew that something was gnawing at me. I didn't like the feeling. Off the field I didn't like myself. On the field, I tried to ignore the waves and echoes of the booing and tried to cope with the general condition of the team, and this was not easy. Production is the basis of morale, and our production wasn't too good. In morale and performance we were swiftly spiraling downward. In 1961 and '62 we finished fifth in our division.

Whether you're a winning team or a losing team, it is always the result of many forces working or failing to work together. A winning team is a marvelous union of the right people and the right energies all flowing in the right direction. A losing team is a similar kind of union moving in the wrong direction. You can blame this guy or that guy or this decision or that decision. But finally it is the chemistry that matters. By the end of the 1962 season no one doubted that the chemistry was definitely wrong. For one thing, a lot of our guys were getting injured. Too many. This is always a bad sign. When a team is going well, it's amazing how few injuries seem to be labeled "serious." A man who wants to play somehow makes it onto the field. He has greater recuperative powers. This was the case with the 49ers in 1970 and '71, when we had tremendous seasons. Almost nobody got "hurt." The same thing happened with the Miami Dolphins in 1973. It's not that the team who has the least injuries has the best chance of winning but rather that the team going the right way has less injuries. A multitude of injuries, on the other hand, is a fairly sure sign that something's wrong.

Looking back I see now that in my own life not only was something wrong, I was actually looking for a way out. This is clearly what I was after when I damn near killed myself in a car early in 1963. If things had been going right, I probably wouldn't have been on a collision course, or out drinking as heavily as I was, and if I hadn't been out drinking I probably wouldn't have been late coming home, and if I hadn't been late coming home, well . . . it astounds me how much planning went into this so-called accident.

The Only Thing I Gained Was Weight

7 IT WAS THE FIRST WEEK in May. I had been at the golf links all afternoon, then spent a few hours in a bar in Redwood City. I lived nearby, in Menlo Park, about thirty miles down the Peninsula from San Francisco. It was after midnight when I started home, alone, and not very alert. Menlo Park isn't what you'd call a fast town. It closes up early, so the streets were empty. I had it all to myself, but that still wasn't enough room. Near the edge of town the street I was following angled sharply to the left, past a cemetery, heading toward the foothills. I say *sharply* because it seemed sharp at the time. It was about a three-degree curve. Even that was more than I could handle.

Just as I reached this curve, two headlights flashed in my rearview. For an instant I thought they were in front of me. In the moment of confusion, my car swerved into some gravel. I tried to right it. The next thing I knew I was out of control, clawing at the wheel. Veering left, the car cut across the road at thirty miles an hour, through the wire and picket fence bordering the cemetery. I was face to face with the biggest goddamn oak tree I had ever seen.

It was as wide as the car and coming right for me, and I couldn't do anything about it. I saw the grain of its bark spreading out in front of me like the side of a barn. I said, "Oh shit!" and lunged to the right, toward the floor mat, to get out from behind the steering wheel. I didn't make it to the floor. My front end powered into the tree, and the right side of my head went into the windshield.

I might have bled to death if another car hadn't pulled up moments later, the car whose lights had flashed in my rearview. Ironically, it was John Ralston, the newly appointed head coach at Stanford, whom I had met once before. I didn't know this at the time. I'd had it. And he didn't know it was me in the car because I was covered with blood and my face and forehead were so torn up, with two big flaps of skin flayed open, no one could have recognized me.

Ralston's wife called the police and an ambulance, and I was rushed to the Stanford Medical Center, where they sewed me up with about a hundred and twenty-eight stitches. I looked so bad at first, people who came to visit me in the emergency ward couldn't tell which victim was me. But I wasn't thinking too much about my face at that point. Something else was injured, and no one had attended to it. My right forearm, my throwing arm, was throbbing.

Soon after I came to, I told the head nurse, "Hey, I think my arm is busted. I'd like to have it x-rayed. It doesn't feel right."

"Can you bend it?" she asked.

I was pretty well anesthetized, with booze. I could

78

bend it and ignore the pain. "Sure I can bend it," I said. "But I know it's broken."

"Well, don't worry about that right now."

I tried to protest. To ease my persistent concern, she gave me a shot, which knocked me out again.

When I woke up the next morning my right arm was in a cast from the wrist to above the elbow. They had x-rayed it and found a fracture. The radius bone was cracked from its impact with the dashboard. I'd have this cast to wear for at least six weeks.

I didn't worry about it too much. They called it a simple fracture, requiring neither surgery nor setting. I figured it would take care of itself and I'd be ready to play when the season started.

After looking at my car I felt lucky to be alive. It was totaled. My head had left an eight-inch hole in the windshield. The front end looked as if it had been flattened in an auto wrecker's press. The great oak itself had absorbed this blow without showing a scratch.

At the end of six weeks they removed the cast, and I immediately began telling everyone my arm never felt better. I started playing golf. Gradually I worked it back into shape. When training camp opened I was throwing the football for the press photographers to prove we were back in business.

It didn't bother me at all until the exhibition season started. Then it hurt a little, like some kind of muscle pull in my forearm. Late in August we were playing Dallas, and during the second quarter my arm started tightening up and made it tough to grip the ball. I couldn't put any speed on the short passes, that extra zip you need to pop the ball in between linebackers. I could still throw long though. After connecting on three long bombs, we were leading at the half, 21-13.

When the medics had examined my arm, Red wouldn't let me go back in to finish the game. A bruise had appeared near my wrist, which we tried to convince ourselves was not related to the fracture. If it was, we were in deep trouble. Billy Kilmer, who had been our back-up quarterback in 1962, had broken his leg in a freeway crash right at the end of the season, a compound fracture, with complications due to infection, and he was going to be out for the year. It was all a foreshadowing of what this whole season would be like.

The next week we played L.A. By this time my arm was really killing me. It ached all the time. I didn't mind the pain that much. Everybody hurts somewhere. But it was affecting my control of the ball. I couldn't grip it hard enough to break a window pane from five feet away. I was getting impatient with myself, and with the doctors, who kept x-raying the arm and diagnosing it as muscle strain, or bruised tendons, or calcium deposits that would soon dissolve and go away. I knew it was more serious than that. In fact, I knew then that it had never healed properly, that it was still broken, or broken again.

In the first two league games we gained a lot of ground, but we couldn't score. Against L.A. I threw for over three hundred yards, but we didn't make a point. We'd get up next to the goal line, and I couldn't put enough speed on the ball for those short, quick end-zone passes. By the third game, against Minnesota, I couldn't throw it ten yards without a searing ache along my forearm. So I was throwing as little as possible (the less I threw it, the longer it would take the defense to find out what I couldn't do), and I was running with the ball. In the second quarter I called a pass play, dropped back to throw, and realized I would never be able to reach my receiver; by the time I spotted him he had run about twenty yards, which was beyond my range. It was infuriating. I ducked and started running, and that was the play that settled the matter.

The only times I have ever been hurt bad on a football field were when I was running with the ball. I never learned how to protect myself, and I always felt I was out of my area, on unfamiliar ground, where I didn't recognize the patterns around me. It's the same sometimes with running backs who find themselves throwing a pass. You can see the uncertain or even terrified look, as they stare wildly around for someone to get the ball to. The men rushing at them are the same men who hit them when they're going through the line, but the pattern is different. You get out of your area and suddenly you realize, Jesus, a man could get *hurt* around here! It happened to me on that unintentional running play. Somebody hit me from the side, got me a perfect lick on my right forearm. The ball flew about ten feet over my head. They recovered it, and I went out of the game, and out of the 1963 season.

This time the x-rays showed a hairline crack where the fracture had been. Scar tissue inside had been irritated. That, and some hemorrhaging, had led to the soreness. If it hadn't been broken before, that blow in the Minnesota game took care of it. They immobilized my arm with another cast to insure complete and permanent healing.

It was supposed to be on there for six weeks. In fact, I was out for the remaining eleven games. It was the worst

81

season the 49ers ever had as a team — two wins and twelve losses — and it was a terrible season for me. The one thing I wanted to do most, the one thing I felt truly fulfilled doing, I couldn't do, and I did not then have the resources to cope with the situation. So I became totally nonproductive. I had all losses and no wins. The only thing I gained was weight. I went from 200 up to 225. I started drinking too much, sopping up everything in town, abusing my friends, and raising enough hell in public places to gain a solid reputation as a wild-ass drunk.

During games, Hickey put me in the spotters' box upstairs, on the other end of the telephones, and I would sit up there watching my team lose ball games. I was sitting in the spotters' box the day we played the Giants in New York City, and I watched Tittle finally even up the score with the 49ers for the way he had been treated there.

I knew Y.A. wanted that game worse than anything he'd ever wanted in his life. Since he'd left we had only played the Giants once, in a 1962 exhibition game in San Francisco, and we beat them bad. The 1963 game was probably going to be his last shot at our team. He gave it everything he had, and he did it. They beat us, 42-14. Tittle didn't let up until the final second. At one point, late in the fourth quarter, he dropped back to throw a pass, and the referee called a fifteen-yard penalty against the Giants. Y.A. tore off his helmet, threw it at the ground, and started kicking it around the field like a soccer ball. He was yelling at the ref, and I was sitting up in the spotters' box thinking, "Well, for Christ sake, Tittle! You're ahead by twenty-eight points. What the hell else do you want? There's only two minutes left to play!"

What he wanted was a 38-point lead. Or 48 points. He

82

told me later that if they'd been ahead by 100, he would have been mad because they didn't have 101.

After the game he decided to come back to the 49er locker room to see his old buddies. He hadn't come to see any of us before the game, but here he came with his twenty-eight points under his belt, still wearing his uniform, wanting to shake hands and talk about old times. And gloat — was the way it looked to me. I was in a dark mood anyway, not being able to play, and having to just sit there and watch my team get whipped so badly. I was overweight and pissed off at the world. I saw Tittle's blue Giants' jersey, his white football pants; I saw his bald head under the ceiling lights and that squint you can never quite interpret. I didn't believe his false humility. He was coming back here to rub it in.

I said, "Tittle, you sonofabitch, nobody in this locker room wants to talk to you. Why don't you get the hell out of here!"

His narrow eyes widened just a hair. His mouth froze. He looked suddenly furious, as if he was going to leap at me. The truth was, he was deeply injured by this greeting. I don't know what he expected from the team he had just demolished, but he didn't expect that. His feelings were hurt, because the way Tittle saw it — and the way he remembers this incident — he was coming back there to welcome us to New York City. We were kind of like kinfolks visiting from out of town. Before the game he was so wound up and bulging with revenge, he couldn't talk to anyone, couldn't eat, or do anything but fidget waiting for the game to start. He was just generally fearful of what might happen if he made contact with anyone on the 49er team before the kick-off. Tittle is a highly superstitious person. When he was with the 49ers he would always sit in the same seat in the bus riding to the games; he would fight a man for that seat. He would wear the same clothes on the day of a game, and during the game he always wore these old high-top shoes he had started out with at LSU, he never would switch over to the low-cutters. So seeing his opponents before that game would have absolutely thrown him into sweat. But now that the game was behind us, he was ready to spend some time with his former teammates. In his own mind, he genuinely wanted to say hello.

Well, my mood was such, and his pride was such, that there wasn't going to be any more communication on the subject. Four more years would pass before we would settle this. Y.A. filed my outburst away for future reference. We glared at each other for a few seconds. Then I got up and walked out of the 49ers locker room. He said a few words to a couple of other people, then he left hurriedly too.

A New Set of Tools

8 IF THERE WAS any advantage to my broken arm and the season I spent on the phones, it was the time this gave me to think. It echoed that period when I was benched as a junior at Stanford. I had a whole year to rethink what I was doing, to ask myself why, in seven seasons, I had not been as productive as I thought I should be. I had been down on everything because I wasn't *cause* of anything. I was total *effect*. And I was the one who had made it that way. I could not blame my frame of mind on the coaches or on bad breaks. I began looking around at other people I admired who were succeeding in their own fields of endeavor, and I saw that they all shared at least one thing in common: they were capable of *making* things go well. They did not make it or lose it because they got a break. They made it because when the break came they were ready. They went into the ball game and took things over. Now I had been able to do that from time to time myself. But my ability to do so was inconsistent. I had never totally been in control of my abilities. This I knew was where I had to apply more attention.

85

The questions I asked myself were different than they had been in 1955. Instead of, "Should I be playing this game?" it was, "Why am I playing this game, and my life, the way I'm playing it?" But my conclusion was basically the same: a renewed resolve to play as well as I could on the football field. The stakes, of course, were higher. I was nine years older. I was not only trying to find meaning in the game. I had, for better or for worse, chosen football. It was the way I was going to "make it." I was not yet giving much thought to why things off the field still weren't going right. My main concern was what happened between the kick-off and the final gun. I wanted to make it in the league, I wanted to make some money and get ahead in the world. In my eyes then, if I blew it on the football field, I had blown it completely.

Coming into the 1964 season I was a new man. The 49ers had a new coach, Jack Christiansen, who had moved up from assistant coach to take over from Red Hickey midway through the difficulties of 1963. There was also a new young quarterback, named George Mira, from the University of Miami. He was the top college passer in the country in 1963, a slim, intense kid who reminded me of a bullfighter. I knew all too well that hungry look in his eyes. He wanted to play so bad he could taste it. I had plenty of reasons to hustle, to sharpen my game. My arm was completely healed. By mid-season I felt I was playing better than ever before. But that was a building year, for the team, and for me. I was, in many ways, warming up for 1965, which Tittle said later was as good a year as any quarterback could ever hope to have.

Coming from Y.A. that meant more to me than all the

86

awards I won in 1965 or all the statistics that piled up in the NFL record sheets, because he had a tremendous amount to do with whatever I achieved that season. As of 1964 he retired as an active player and returned to San Francisco to coach our offensive backfield. It was more than affection for his old teammates that brought him back to the West Coast. He owned a home in Atherton, and he had an insurance business in Palo Alto. It was a good arrangement all the way around. There were no visible signs that he bore a grudge over our showdown in the locker room or over the rivalry that had sent him — it seemed at the time — into exile. He had led the Giants to three successive Eastern Conference titles. He had another Most Valuable Player trophy standing on his shelf. He had retired a winner and came to camp ready to help the 49ers any way he could. What he brought with him was a lifetime of football knowledge, plus some extremely valuable insights as a result of his combined experience on the West Coast and in New York. He pooled this with what Bill Johnson, now line coach and offensive coordinator, knew about all other aspects of offense, and with what Billy Wilson, who had rejoined the club as an assistant coach, knew about receiving, and they shaped up one of the best systems I've ever seen. In 1965 we led the NFL in points scored and in total yardage gained, and six of us from the offensive team went to the Pro Bowl.

One tends to think that all there is to learn is what he has been taught in his own puddle. In New York Y.A. discovered another whole world of thought about how to coach and organize a team. Vince Lombardi had shaped the Giants' offense in the late fifties, and although he had already moved on to Green Bay, his presence was still

strongly felt when Tittle arrived in New York in 1961. In
my case, Y.A. understood where my mind was at, because
he had been in the same place himself. He came back
understanding both what I did know and a whole bunch
of things I did not know, and he saw how he could help
me and help the team.

Our pass numbering system, for instance, had been
very restrictive. There were certain things we just
couldn't do. I would call a play in the huddle, then as we
lined up over the ball a hole would open somewhere in
the defense, and with the audibles we had to work with, I
just couldn't get to it. We would have two or three pass
audibles for an entire game, and this wasn't enough. Y.A.
knew that our whole pass offense should be audibled.
We began to structure it so that I could call out any play I
wanted to, at the line of scrimmage, and the players
would understand this easily. We developed nine basic
patterns. I could call on any one of these nine with a
single number and everyone on the team would be ready.

Previously we were devising different audibles every
week, trying to second-guess the other team's defense.
Our main purpose was to use audibles to get ourselves
out of a bad situation. The most I could do was alter the
route of a receiver or a running back. We did not yet
have a structure that took into consideration a thorough
understanding of the defense and defensive weaknesses.
If I saw a defensive formation I had not anticipated, my
thinking would be something like, "Oh shit. We can't do
it. Now what else can we do?" And I would come up
with something out of the blue. Or my mind would click
back to a play the coach had said would be good to call in
such and such a situation. But if it didn't work, I would

be frustrated, not only because the play failed, but because I didn't feel I had the best tools to work with.

When that happens, when you're changing plays and the change doesn't improve anything, the linemen get frustrated too. They're thinking, "Screw it. Why doesn't he just run the goddamn play?" Pretty soon their confidence in the quarterback diminishes, and everyone is yelling at everyone else about what's going wrong.

In 1965 we stopped using audibles to get out of bad situations and began using them to create good situations. Tittle brought some sanity and some logic to the whole system, and I could now call anything I wanted, based on whatever I perceived in the defensive setup. It was a kind of tool that allowed my abilities to expand greatly. It was like I had been trying to travel on roller skates and had suddenly inherited a sports car.

We would study game films with this in mind, looking for specific situations — weaknesses or tendencies in the defense — and then apply our audible system to these situations. So that once the game began, I'm in the huddle calling a play and already thinking, "Okay, look for this defense. If it isn't there, run the play. If it is there, go to this other play." Then when we get to the line, and I see the situation we have all been prepared for appearing on the field, I call the audible. Everyone on the team recognizes it, they are expecting a really big play. The linemen are thinking, "Baby doll!" they're licking their chops with the feeling that this has got to be it, the one we've been waiting for. When this kind of planning began to work consistently, it filled the whole offensive team with a new kind of enthusiasm and confidence.

The way it worked was simple, like so many other

things in life that seem simple and obvious after someone works it out so that others understand how they function. In the huddle I might call a play like, "Brown, right. Blunt, thirty-six. On two." BROWN designated one of four basic formations; in this case the fullback lined up behind the quarterback, with the halfback to the side away from the tight end and the receiver and flanker back split wide. RIGHT meant that this Brown formation would line up to the right side (LEFT simply reversed it, putting the tight end on the left side of the line, etc.). BLUNT designated a series of plays that sent the halfback blocking the weakside linebacker, everyone else blocking man on man, and the fullback carrying the ball into the line. The first number referred to the ball carrier. In this formation the fullback happens to be the number-three back. The second number is the hole he aimed for. Holes on the left side of the line were even-numbered; on the right side, odd-numbered. In this play the fullback would be heading for the number-six hole, just outside the left tackle. The last number, two, is the snap count.

When we got to the line of scrimmage I would scan the defensive setup. If I wanted to change the play I would yell out the snap count — in this case, "Two." That tells the other players that the next numbers I call will be a new play. I might call out, "Two. Fifty-three," and call it loud to both sides of the line, and then start the count. If I'm not going to change the play, I still call an audible — a phony one — which starts with a different snap count than the one I gave in the huddle. "Three. Eighty-five," yelling that to both sides of the lines. But when the others guys hear, "Three," they stop listening, because they know we're going with the original play.

90

While the game was in progress, Y.A. would be upstairs in the spotters' box and talking to the bench. From my point of view he was the best possible guy to have on the phones. He'd been there. He knew the difference between looking at it from the press box and looking at it from behind the center. And believe me, these are two completely different perspectives. He sent nothing but useful information down to the bench. Certain suggestions aren't much good at all, things like, "Throw it to Casey, he's hot!" I'm two feet away from Casey every minute of the afternoon, and I already know if he's hot or not. But there are other things I'm not so sure about, such as what exactly is going on in the defensive secondary. If it's a running play I can usually see it for myself, because they're close enough. But a pass play is harder for a quarterback to follow. The secondary will try to cover their defense by giving you a picture that shifts as soon as the ball is snapped. Tittle knew what I *expected* should be happening. He could see whether we had figured it right or not, and if it had changed we could talk about how to beat it. Any information like that would just add to my confidence level in calling the next series of plays. When you set out to exploit a weakness in a defense, you like to know that what you expect to see has a good chance of being there.

Until that season, exploiting the defensive secondary had been one of our biggest problems. Specifically, handling the blitzes. In a blitz, one or more linebackers, and sometimes a defensive back, join in the rush on the passer. Historians of the game say the blitz was a 49er invention, first used in 1957 against the New York Giants. Maybe our defense invented it, but until 1965 our offense

91

didn't have an effective method for picking it up. It was the quarterback's job to decide, in the seconds before the snap, is this linebacker going to come or is he not going to come? If I thought he was going to come, and I called a blitz audible, this would break up the pattern I had called in the huddle. But if he *did* come, and I had not called the audible, he was going to catch me behind the line. Or I might sense a blitz coming and call an audible to take advantage of it; then, instead of rushing me, the linebacker would drop right into the hole where I wanted to throw the ball, which meant I had nowhere to go with it because I had audibled for this blitz and the two backs had stayed in to cover it, thus my alternate receivers weren't out in the pattern but standing back there patting me on the ass.

We were so vulnerable to the blitz that some weeks, in desperation, we would keep our backs in on every play just to be ready for it. But that would cut down the effectiveness of our whole pass offense. In short, we just weren't set up to cope with the blitz. I was involved in a continual guessing game, which took a lot of my attention away from where it should have been — downfield. Worse than that, I was getting caught a lot, and the more I got caught, the more they blitzed us.

All of this changed when we adopted the "swing pickup," which only three or four other teams were using at that time. It meant the fullback was always responsible for the outside linebacker to the strong side, and the halfback was always responsible for the other outside linebacker, and the center was responsible for the middle linebacker. Any time one of these guys decided to blitz, they were covered. No matter where else the halfback was going, he took a look at that linebacker first. If he was coming, the halfback got him. If he wasn't coming, the halfback went on out into his pattern. In this new system, the way we had the plays designed, even if a linebacker did come through, there was nothing to panic about. Somebody had missed a block, that's all. You have to give the defense a play once in a while, but know why.

Soon the situation completely reversed itself. It got to the point where other teams would not blitz us. We had learned how to *use* the blitz as an offensive tool. Later on in my career I actually loved to see a blitz coming. It meant I had a receiver out there man to man in the defensive backfield. With a little bit of time any pro quarterback can beat a man-to-man defense. What we would do, we would intimidate the other team to blitz, and then when they did we'd burn them.

When this started to happen, sportswriters were reporting that I had become a master of the blitz. *You can't get Brodie on a blitz,* they would say, *he knows when they're coming and when they're not coming,* as if I had developed some sixth sense for the blitzers. This made me chuckle. They were giving me credit for something I wasn't really doing. It was the whole offensive structure that made this possible. If anyone deserved credit, it was the backs, who had to take that larger responsibility and be flexible enough and knowledgeable enough to make accurately those split second decisions.

Responsibility was the key word. The logic and clarity of the system let each guy know just what was expected of him and of everyone else. Nobody put the finger on the quarterback unless he was responsible. Each offensive

93

lineman knew exactly where the quarterback was supposed to be on every play. Bill Johnson had worked it all out in meticulous detail. Y.A. had contributed a whole lot of theory; Bill had worked out its application. Y.A. and I were in such close accord on all this that by midseason he could predict, from his vantage point in the spotters' booth, 95 percent of my calls.

For the first time in my experience all the responsibilities were laid out clearly. We each knew what our jobs were, and thus each man could gauge what he had done or failed to do and whether a problem was his or someone else's or the group's. When we took a game apart, took particular plays apart afterward, it was simple to get the mistakes corrected, and it was never an attempt to prove one man wrong but to keep the team moving right.

John David

9 IN THIS ATMOSPHERE everyone's performance improved, and we had some outstanding performers to begin with. Bernie Casey had been a premier receiver in the league for four years. The previous season he had been joined by David Parks, from Texas Tech, the first player picked in the 1964 college draft and a Pro Bowl choice after his rookie year. By the end of 1965 David was the NFL's leading pass receiver, with a phenomenal season total of eighty catches. He and Gene Washington, who came to the 49ers four years later, are the two best receivers I have ever seen. Ken Willard, the All-American from North Carolina, was a rookie fullback in 1965. John David Crow had just been traded from St. Louis. And in the offensive line we had five men who made All-Pro at one time or another during their careers: Howard Mudd, John Thomas, Bruce Bosley, Len Rohde, and Walter Rock.

For me, the man who most represented the feeling on the team that year was John David Crow. He had won the Heisman Trophy at Texas A & M and been a star running back with the St. Louis Cardinals. The year he made All Pro — 1960 — he gained over a thousand yards, which up to that time very few rushers had accomplished. You can tell a lot about a running back from how the guys on defense regard him. Our linemen who had played against John David would talk about him with nothing but respect: "Man, when that guy runs, he goes right over the *top* of you!" His knees gave him trouble for a couple of years, though, and things at St. Louis had not been going too well for him. When he got traded to San Francisco he was delighted. He liked it on the West Coast. Once he got involved with our new offensive system, he liked that too. He loved it. He helped the rest of us appreciate how functional it was. "Godamighty," he would say, "I can't believe how simple it is out here. Back at St. Louis we used to spend two and three years just learning the numbers. We had triple wings, and double reverses, a whole lot of fancy stuff Pop Ivy had brought down with him from when he coached in the Canadian League. I finally understood why they used twelve players up there. They keep one extra guy on the field just to pick up the fumbles."

John David comes from Springhill, Louisiana, 6-3, 225 pounds, a tough, hard-hitting ballplayer. His main job with the 49ers was blocking back and secondary receiver, and he gave it everything. He was one of the most intelligent players I have ever known. He understood our system and why his role had to be what it was; and he was totally committed to contributing whatever he could to the overall performance of the team. He had an attitude toward the game that was truly inspirational for everyone else who played with him. Here's the kind of thing he would do. In 1968, our tight end, Bob Windsor,

96

got drafted into the army. John David was asked if he would switch positions. His attitude was, Hell, if that's where I can do the most good, that's where I'll play. Now he had been playing halfback for his entire career, and he had piled up a total of nearly 5000 yards gained rushing, which is something of a milestone. He was about thirty-seven yards short. After he played tight end all that season, the coaches decided to give him a chance to pick up the remaining yardage. But John said, No, he didn't want to do it that way, he didn't want to make a production out of it. "If I have to run the ball just so I can get into some record book, I'd rather keep the 4967 which I know I got by playing football. It'd be nice to make 5000, but it ain't that big a deal."

John David was just as tough a tight end as he had been a running back. I can remember a game in 1968 when we were playing Los Angeles and trying to figure a way to block Deacon Jones, one of the biggest defensive ends in the league, and also one of the fastest. The coaches came up with the idea of putting John David in motion so that he could kind of sideswipe Deacon — who outweighed him by fifty pounds — just as the ball was snapped.

John lined up wide to the right, out there with the flanker back. As I started my count he started moving in toward the line, and just as the ball moved he came powering across to crack down on Deacon, who had his eye on me, not on the flankers. He didn't see John David coming, but he was so fast that John David got him in the small of the back. Deacon said, "Jesus Christ, what was *that?*"

He looked around and saw John David getting up. "Was that you?"

John said, "Yeah, yeah, yeah. But it wasn't my fault, it wasn't my fault. The coaches called it."

Deacon didn't like that strategy at all. But I called for it again, on the next play, figuring that if he got hit once more by a man in motion he would be looking over that way for the rest of the game. That tiny distraction was all our tackle needed to get a good piece of him — which is the way it finally worked out.

The second time John David landed a solider blow, and Deacon was so pissed off he was ready to fight. "Brodie," he said to me, "you call that play one more time, I'm going to kill you!"

"Hey, don't look at me," I said. "The coaches sent it in. We're not trying to hurt you. We're just trying to get your ass out of there any way we can."

Deacon said, "Crow, did you think that up?"

John David said, "Hell, no, I didn't think it up. It was Tittle. Tittle put that together."

Deacon said, "Well, bu-u-u-l-l-*shit!* You'd better not do it again."

"I'll tell you what, Deacon," I said, "you stop hittin' me on top of the head the way you like to do, and I won't call that play anymore."

He grumbled something and walked away. In the huddle John David said to me, "If it's all the same to you, I'd just as soon you'd line me up over on the left side for a while. There's a guy over here on the right side who is just a little bit pissed. And I don't think I've got my gun on me."

So I called a few formation lefts, but then I got to focusing on other parts of the game. John David's request kind of slipped my mind, and I called another formation right,

98

which put him in front of Jack Pardee, the Rams outside linebacker. Deacon looked at John David, then he looked at Pardee and growled, "Switch, Jack."

He lined up right over Crow. When the ball was snapped, Deacon came up swinging as hard as he could swing. John just ducked a little and drove under him with his helmet. He bopped Deacon square on the chin and dropped him again. Then he got out of there fast. He came loping back to the huddle, half pleased with himself and half begging me, "Jesus Christ, I never saw a man that mad in my life. He's gonna murder me next time. I ain't shittin' ya, John. Keep me on the *other side*."

John David was my roommate in 1965 and for the next three years he played in San Francisco. He's another man I'm much indebted to for enlarging my grasp of the game. Like Tittle, he broke everything down in terms of workability — which was my main interest too. We were exactly the same age, we enjoyed a lot of the same things — good beer, good restaurants, good football — and we would spend hours talking about backfield play. We would get so enthused in these discussions we'd go out at three in the afternoon and get back at midnight, talking intently the whole time, drinking beer, and mapping out receiver routes.

Until I got to know John David I had not really seen the game from a halfback's point of view: what was most important to him about the timing of a play or the pattern in a sequence of plays. Hearing him talk I soon began to see that I had a lot more to learn about the workability of other positions and the need to see the game through the

99

eyes of each guy on the team. With John David's encouragement I began to approach other players in ways I had been reluctant to do before, walking up to a guard like Howard Mudd, for instance, and asking him why he made this move on such and such a play — not to challenge him but just to find out what was going through his mind.

John David had broken down every aspect of the game that related to his position. Each week he would take apart the moves of all the linebackers we'd be facing to figure out how specific plays could take advantage of specific drops he knew they'd be making. He would tell me when, as a halfback, he liked to hit a certain hole, where he liked to stand in relation to the scrimmage line from one play to the next. He had a reason for every route he ran. Just take the example of a hook pattern. He had three or four ways he liked to run a hook. He would make sure I understood each one so that as soon as he started his route I knew what he was going to do. He would tell me precisely when to anticipate his cut and which shoulder to throw the ball to. We would go over every one of his routes that way.

The first time we played the Rams in 1965, at the L.A. Coliseum, we were ahead 14-10 in the middle of the first half. I had just thrown the ball to John David. He came back to the huddle and said, "Call that same play, sixty-five. I'm cutting right through the linebackers, but I'll cut underneath Eddie Meador" — their free safety. "I've got to have it somewhere between the thirty and the forty," he said, "on their end of the field. That's the only way I can run that far and score on it. If I get it on this side of the field, they'll run me to the ground."

I heard the "between the thirty and the forty" part of

100

this plan but didn't hear the "their end of the field" part too well. A while later we were back there between *our* thirty and forty, and I asked him, "How's it doin'?" He said sort of tentatively, "Okay," which meant he didn't much want to run the ball that far. But I went ahead and called, "Brown, right, sixty-five, halfback up," and said to him, "John, you know what to do."

And he did. He went straight up the field and cut underneath Meador. I was getting a strong rush from the Rams front line, but because I knew so well what John David was going to do, because he had described it so exactly to me, I could let the ball go before he made his last cut. When I threw I didn't have to see the catch to know that it would be complete.

He took it over his shoulder and got all the way down to the one-yard line before they tackled him. He fell into the end zone for a score, and he was so goddamn tired he could barely get up. He hadn't really looked forward to battling it for sixty yards. But he did it. John David always got the job done.

TIMING

I ALMOST ALWAYS knew, an instant
after the ball was gone, what was going to happen,
whether it would be complete or incomplete or intercepted. It wasn't the feel of the throw itself that told me
but how accurately I had foreseen the path of my receiver. If you wait until you see how he's going to break,
you have waited too long. Too many people can get to
the ball. You have to envision where he'll be and where
you're going to hit him before he makes his last move.
You can't predict how he's going to come out of it. He can
get bumped or lose his footing. But I would know, as
soon as he *came* out of it, whether or not the pass was
going to be complete. If he made his move the way we
both expected, I knew he had it.

Things liked that are what account for the quick release. The whiplike arm quarterbacks are so often
praised for isn't enough by itself. What counts is the combination of quickness of body and the decision to get it
done. It's something that arises from the whole structure
of the offense. The ability to throw quickly is like the

102

most visible product of a machine that is working well, rather than the opposite idea, that a well-thrown ball is what makes the machine go.

Another thing about the timing of a throw — there's no use hurrying up to get ready and then find your receiver just moving off the line of scrimmage. Coaches are obsessed with stopwatches. A guy gets back and sets up in 1.8 seconds. Another guy gets back in 1.5 seconds. The coaches say, "Holy Jesus, look at that guy's drop!" Yet it doesn't make that much difference. The receiver still has to run his pattern. You get back there in record time, and what do you do? You've got so much time you start noticing the linemen, and your attention is diverted from where it ought to be. What's important is to *comfortably* get back into position — and you can do that in 2, 2.5 seconds — in time to release the ball at just the right moment and not give the play away while your receiver is still making his moves.

An Ancient Feud

10 NINETEEN SIXTY-FIVE happened to be one of the few years we beat Los Angeles two league games out of two. If nothing else at all had happened that season, this in itself would have been enough to celebrate. We had a rivalry going with the Rams that went back to 1950. It goes back a lot farther than that, if you want to take into account how northern California and southern California have been bad-mouthing each other since before the Gold Rush. It's no surprise that the first two pro football teams on the West Coast should take special pleasure in trying to plow each other under.

In my seventeen years with the 49ers we played L.A. fifty-one times, counting all exhibition and league games. It never made any difference who was the underdog or the favorite. There was no way anyone could predict the outcome. It was like the Stanford-California game — with real emotion behind every match, sometimes more emotion than genuine preparation for the contest.

The exhibition game, which we played traditionally in the L.A. Coliseum to wind up the exhibition season, might as well have been a regular league game. Whatever the exhibition's stated purpose, all of that was forgotten. We came at each other ready for bear. And the league games themselves — somehow they were more than league games. This was a competition unto itself. No matter what else we did, we had to beat Los Angeles. Something about the Rams made us want to take them apart. Even their helmets pissed us off, with those ram's-horn stripes curling back over the ears. I can remember Red Hickey telling us before one game, "Everybody in Hollywood is a phony." That didn't necessarily relate to the quality of a team that happened to have its franchise in southern California. But it was exactly the kind of thing we wanted to hear. Any reason we could find to have a go at them was just that much more fuel for the fire.

I myself was not born with this attitude. It was something I had to learn if I was going to survive as a 49er. I learned it early, the first time we played them after I joined the team. It was the exhibition game in 1957. I watched it all from the bench and afterward said hello to a friend of mine, Jon Arnett, a rookie halfback who had just joined the Rams. We had competed against each other when he was playing for USC, and we had played on the same College All-Star team just a few months earlier. He played a great game against the 49ers, running punts and kick-offs back, establishing himself as a new celebrity. I went over to congratulate him and to ask him how he liked the Rams. He asked me how I was liking San Francisco, etc. When I got back to the 49er locker room, you'd think I had just shaken hands with Satan. They all came at me at once.

"Why don't you go give the guy a great big kiss?"

"That little sumbitch damn near killed us, that's all! He ain't nobody's friend!"

"What the fuck football team you belong to anyhow?"

The rivalry was fierce. But it wasn't vicious. In those fifty-one games, which were all hard-fought, very few fights ever broke out on the field. Here's the kind of thing that would happen. Once, while John David was running the ball about forty-five yards, down to their six, there was a lot of open field action on the play, and somebody took this opportunity to get even with somebody else. Tempers were already hot. Suddenly Merlin Olsen and Deacon Jones and three or four other guys about that size were all on our side of the field. It just turned into a free-for-all. I saw John David with the ball standing way down by the goal line next to Eddie Meader, L.A.'s defensive back, watching the action. He told me later he had said to Eddie, "You really feel like getting into all that? Why don't we let those guys fight it out, and we'll just sit here and cool it."

Which they did.

We actually respected one another a lot as ballplayers. Over the years I made several good friends in Los Angeles (although I learned to keep it to myself around game time). We also had some good times out on the field — like the day Howard Mudd decided to play a trick on Merlin and Deacon. One of the reasons those two guys were so good, they were always looking for any kind of an edge, any advantage. They noticed every little thing that happened around them — which is what led Howard to think this up in the first place.

Just as we came to the line, Howard whispered to me,

"What's the count?" As if trying to conceal my answer, I whispered back, "One." Now the rest of the guys were in on this. If they hadn't been, they would all have jumped up saying, "What? What? I thought you said it was on two?" It *was* on two. But Merlin, who played opposite Howard, had picked up the whispered message and he had passed it on to Deacon, and a count before the ball was snapped, both of them were moving.

Merlin caught himself but couldn't hold his position without crossing the scrimmage line, so he just rolled over. Then Deacon fell over Merlin, and they went into a kind of tumbling act that left Deacon flat on his back when the play started. Howard got to laughing so much that he fell down too, fell right over on top of the other two guys. They all sort of canceled each other out, and we went on to make about eight yards on the play.

The first league game we played against L.A. in 1965, in the Coliseum, we won 45-21. When we played the second time, in San Francisco, they were after us. Their honor was at stake. It didn't make any difference who was ahead of who in the league standings — neither one of us was standing very high at the time — it was just the Rams coming north to clean house on the 49ers. That's the way they saw it. And it was a tight ball game all the way. What won it for us was all these new ingredients I have described that came together in 1965: the swing pickup, easy-to-handle audibles, John David's fire, outstanding receivers, and an offensive line that could hold their rushers back long enough for me to throw. During the middle sixties the Rams had the best defensive line in the league. I have never seen four men of that size all

together in one place anywhere else in my life. The ends
were Deacon Jones and Lamar Lundy. The tackles were
Merlin Olsen and Roger Brown. Those four gentlemen
could make things happen play after play after play.
They put any offense to the test. When we could move
the ball against those guys, I knew we were cooking.

During the first half the Rams defense blitzed us a few
times. When they did, our backs stayed in and picked up
the blitzers. And Rich Petitbon, one of their backs,
would tip us off by the way he set his legs, so we could
see it coming before the ball was snapped. When linebackers are rushing, there's nobody to hold up the receivers; they can get downfield fast. Because we had simple
audibles to come to, whenever we saw a blitz taking
shape, we could pick it up and quickly put receivers into
the secondary, where they would be covered man to man
and thus easy to get the ball to.

That was the trick, to get one of our receivers into a
man-on-man situation. We had so many good receivers
that season, there was no way L.A. could cover all of them
adequately on every play once we had their defense figured.

By the fourth quarter they were down basically to two
defenses. Either they were doubling up on the weak
side, playing three men on John David Crow and the split
end, David Parks, or they were doubling up on the strong
side, playing three on two against the flanker and Bernie
Casey, the tight end. I had stopped using audibles, because all we had to do to know which of these formations
they'd use was to watch Eddie Meador. Eddie was an
outstanding safety, the kind of back who loved to be
where the action was, but he was so impulsive a

ballplayer that he would commit himself early, at the snap, and he would key which way the defense planned to go — the strong side or the weak side. He had learned to depend a lot on the Rams' pass rush, which was so effective that ordinarily he could *afford* to commit early. But our line wasn't letting them through. I had enough time to watch the patterns form. The receivers watched Eddie too. We were running combination patterns, so that whichever side they doubled on, I just threw to the opposite side of the field.

At the end of the third quarter L.A. was leading 27-13. But none of our guys were panicking about the score. We knew what we could do, we knew we had time to catch up. Early in the fourth quarter we scored on a pass play, making it 27-20. Then, with about nine minutes to go in the game, we got the ball back on our own thirty-five, and we started moving it down the field, just putting together all our own abilities and all the details we had gathered in the first three quarters of the game.

Monty Stickles caught the first pass, a short one in the flat. David Parks caught a short pass to the outside for eight yards and a first down. Four men had to force him out of bounds. It always took that many men, or more, to stop David.

John David Crow made six yards on a draw play. Then Bernie Casey caught the ball for another first down. I threw an incomplete to Bernie, then completed a pass to Ken Willard, which picked up twenty-one yards. A short hitch to Bernie brought us to the L.A. fourteen. After I threw an incomplete to Willard in the end zone, we had a third down and about three to go for a first.

Crow came back to the huddle and said it was a perfect

time to call for an out-and-up, a play that would send David Parks faking one of his short routes to the outside, then cutting past his defender and heading for the goal line. To make it work Crow had to be able to occupy the outside linebacker, who otherwise would be over there helping the cornerback cover the short-out pattern. But Crow had the knack for knowing when one of his own moves would work best. This was just the kind of thing he and I would talk about in our late-night, beer-drinking conversations. David Parks would come along with us a lot of the time. He was just as meticulous as Crow when it came to taking apart the routes he ran and relating them to everything else on the field. Those two would map out complementary routes such as this one, designed to siphon off defenders from the primary receiver. Our long preparatory talks cut down the talk on the field to one or two words. In this case all John David actually said was, "Now," and we knew what he meant.

Since Parks had just caught that sideline pass for eight yards, the cornerback wasn't going to lay back and let him catch another one in front of him. He could only lay back if he could depend on the linebacker to help out — in which case the cornerback would never have to commit himself on what appeared to be a short-out pattern. But the linebacker was not going to be helping, because I had thrown enough balls to John David in the flat that the linebacker had to stay honest and stay on Crow's route — a ten-yard route he could run several ways. That meant the cornerback would be playing Parks man to man.

And that was just the way it worked. Parks went for the sideline. The cornerback moved in to cover. Parks made his move, shot past him to catch the ball in the end zone. With the extra point the score was tied 27-27.

110

After kick-off Los Angeles had the ball on their own twenty. Roman Gabriel threw three incompletes in a row, and they had to punt out, which gave us the ball back on our own forty-nine, with three minutes and thirty-seven seconds showing on the clock.

When we got into the huddle, I remember Crow urging us all, "Now *look!* We have come too *far* to tie this god-damn game! Everybody just pick up and do his own thing, and we'll git it!"

It was a voice full of fire yet absolutely in control, and it set the mood for our final drive. This was what made that 1965 offense so effective. We could play adventurously, or we could play conservatively, but either way we still played aggressively. You might take a bigger risk passing into the middle of the defensive secondary than you would running the fullback into the line; there is a much higher risk of losing the ball. But because the blunt is a more conservative play, that doesn't mean anyone can afford to hold back — which is what I have seen happen when a team is more concerned with *preserving* something than continuing to *pursue* something.

We had made that last score on a series of pass plays. Now it was time to move it on the ground. Willard ran a blunt up to their forty-four, and ran it again up to the forty for a first down. John David dove into the line, and somebody went for his face mask, which got L.A. penalized fifteen yards. Willard powered through for four more and then made four again. John David picked up four more through the middle, putting the ball on L.A.'s fifteen-yard line.

By this time about thirty seconds remained in the game. People in the stands were going wild, yelling for somebody to call a time out. The coaches and guys on the bench were yelling for a time out. Then somebody on the field actually did call for time. The ref started to stop the clock and I yelled at him, "Who the hell called time out?"

Somebody yelled back at me, "For Christ sake, the clock's running down!"

I said, "Goddamn it, I'll call time out!" I know what's going on! I'm the only one who *can* call it!

"Ref," I yelled. "Start up the clock!"

Well, that just about drove everybody in the stands and on the sidelines into a frenzy. We stood around while the clock ticked off almost twenty seconds — all the way down to nine. *Then* I called for time.

Tommy Davis, our place kicker, came in. He put a twenty-two-yard field goal between the posts, giving us a three-point lead with six seconds remaining. A Rams back took the kick-off to midfield, then time ran out. We had the ball game, 30-27, and we had the Rams two league games out of two, which had not happened since 1960, and as of the time this book was written hasn't happened since.

THE HUDDLE

PART OF WHAT came clear to me in 1965 was the mastery of the huddle. It is all related. The offensive structure helped me visualize the game. The logic of it gave me a sense of certainty to take into the huddle.

No other game — except Rugby — has anything quite like the huddle. Baseball players stand yards apart throughout the inning and have to yell their messages. Basketball players put their heads together during time outs and at half and quarter breaks. But every thirty seconds, football players cluster up close for their brief, secret conference. The huddle is its own little world. One night the NFL wired my shoulder pads with a remote microphone for a special film they were putting together. Among other things, they wanted to catch the intimacy of the huddle. Most of those parts of the game had to be edited out. At least the soundtrack had to be edited very tightly.

All sorts of things happen. Usually it's dead quiet in the huddle. Sometimes everyone is yammering at once, stepping on feet, cracking jokes. That's where the players do their vomiting and the pissing in their pants. We got into a huddle once and I was about to say, "Okay, let's have a go at it," which was kind of our war cry that season, when I noticed that one of our rookie guards had a stream of urine running out of his pants and down onto the ground. Ken Willard could mimic me perfectly. He said, "It looks like he's already *had* a go at it." Someone else cracked, "Who *said* this game is important?"

The huddle is almost a game in itself. I have heard hours of talk on the shape of the huddle, how to break the huddle, the importance of hurrying back into the huddle, or out of the huddle. Coaches all have theories about it. So do the various players. A receiver, for instance, after he has finished running his pattern, will usually take his time getting back; he's resting, so he walks slow to the huddle, knowing they won't start the clock until he has crossed the scrimmage line. Some running backs feel the same way. When the ball is down, they're dead. Their rest time starts then. So on the way back, and while they're in the huddle, they're conserving every ounce of energy for the next burst. A lot of offensive linemen are different though. They get started, they want to keep going. The play's over, they're jumping right back into the huddle, full of vinegar and ready to cut loose *now.*

For the quarterback the tempo of the huddle is a crucial factor in managing the tempo of the game. He can actually *set* the tempo. If you're stalling, or want the game to slow down, you use every second of huddle time you own. When the game's going your way and you take too long you can lose momentum. Then it's important for a team to hurry back, get a play and keep it all moving, keep the continuity flowing and don't give the defense time to breathe. Keep your team's mind on attack and on scoring more points, not on the quarter, or the weather, or the other guy's score, not on anything but this play, boom, move it, this play, boom, move it!

The main purpose of the huddle, of course, is that moment of communication when your team's next move is decided. It takes many a quarterback years to reach the point where he owns that moment, the same way he has to own the plays.

When I first started out, in high school, all I knew about the huddle was what I had seen from the outside, watching guys like Bob Celeri at Cal, one of my earliest models. I knew what the motions looked like, and that's about all I could do — go through the motions. Getting it formed up right was very important to me, and looking right, and sounding right. Having something to say was another matter. But whatever I said I wanted it to sound like the right thing too. I felt obliged to give the guys a little pep talk for about five seconds before I called the play. Then I would call it, and clap my hands, and say, "Okay, let's go." Even then I knew that the pep talk and the hand clap was bullshit, and the other guys knew it was bullshit, and it came out as bullshit, and finally I started trying to break the habit. I'd catch myself starting into the pep talk — "Okay, you guys" — and then I'd stop and say, "Oops, sorry, I'm sorry, my fault," and I'd start over, groping around for a play. In high school you were a good play caller if you could simply get one out, that is, just remember the numbers well enough to pick one in the huddle. So I would call a formation, then the number, and with that done I would feel a great relief, like, man, I

115

did it. But we had not yet left the huddle, so it would be up to the line of scrimmage to drop the voice an octave and call it out, whether I knew what I was talking about or not. That's what it meant to be a *leader,* which we were told was another important quality a quarterback should have. This was very much on my mind when I started playing at Stanford, the idea of appearing to be a leader. About half the time this meant a guy who yelled at his players loud enough that the head coach would hear it and walk over to another coach and say hopefully, "By God, that boy's a leader."

I have talked to a lot of young quarterbacks in recent years, and although the game is more sophisticated now at every level than it was twenty years ago, many of the problems are very recognizable to me. Often it is a matter of undoing some preformed notions about what a quarterback should *look like* and giving more thought to what he should *be,* not to worry so much about proper huddle procedure but give more thought to what you honestly want to communicate. At all levels of football — high school, college, and pro — many assignments are missed because players are not listening to or not hearing the quarterback. They are listening to all the formalities he has picked up. This distracts their attention, or they just tune out. If you go into the high school locker room after the game, and the players are just goofing around, the kid never has a communication problem when he says, "Come on over to my house tonight and pick me up at seven and we'll go to the show." It's real simple when you convey the message that way. The other guy will be there.

This is a condition that can continue right on into pro

116

ball. I have seen rookie quarterbacks go into a huddle
with this leadership image in mind, and before they call a
play they have to spend a few seconds chewing everybody out — just from habit. We had a young guy come
down from Washington State a few years back as a second
draft choice. He jogged into his first huddle and said,
"All right! Goddamn it, you guys. Let's get this thing
together!" Bob St. Clair, who had been watching this sort
of routine off and on for ten years — the veteran master
sergeant eyeing the green lieutenant — just muttered at
him, "Oh, fuck you." And the kid wilted. "Okay," he
said. "Okay, I'm sorry."

Although I stepped into a lot of traps in my early years,
I think that's one I avoided. I assumed that what we had
to start with was a group of tough men who were highly
motivated or they wouldn't have been there in the first
place. It wasn't necessary to take a hypodermic needle
and pump them full of "ability." They had that, or they
wouldn't have been drafted to play this game. My first
job was to learn the system the team was using — the play
numbers, the snap counts, the audible patterns, etc. — to
master that, so I could apply this knowledge to the situation on the field and, in those few seconds in the huddle,
get the play out, get it out completely and accurately to
everyone as easily as I could. To the degree that my
thinking was effective and I could do this without self-
consciousness, the other men would listen and grant me
command.

An Offer I
Couldn't Refuse

11 I HAD A LOT of good reasons to stay with the 49ers: John David Crow, David Parks, Bernie Casey, Ken Willard, Howard Mudd, Bill Johnson, etc., etc. We had put together one of the best offensive systems in football, and no one wants to leave all that work and workmanship behind. At the same time, after the '65 season, I knew that my own stock should be going up. I had made All-Pro. I had set an NFL record for passes completed in a single season (242) and had the highest career pass completion average of any pro quarterback in history (57 percent). And it must be said that every working quarterback was intensely aware of the then fantastic sum offered to Joe Namath just the previous year. As a rookie from the University of Alabama joining the New York Jets, Joe had signed for a reputed $400,000 for three years. I can assure you, this starts a man thinking. Here I was, with nine years in the game, and barely making a fourth of that.

When I met that spring with Lou Spadia, the 49ers owner, to discuss my new contract, I told him I thought I

118

should be getting a raise, and that $80,000 sounded about right. Lou agreed about the raise, but not about the figure. He offered me fifty-five, with some incentive bonuses, and I said I'd like ten days to think it over. It was all very friendly. Lou and I have almost always been able to talk in an open and friendly way. In fact, ours is not only the longest continuous relationship I have had with anyone in football (he was general manager of the 49ers when I joined in 1957 and is running the club today), I think we may have set some kind of longevity record: we were both working with the same organization during my seventeen years as a pro.

At any rate, that's where things stood the day Don Klosterman called me from Houston in May of 1966 saying he and Bud Adams, owner of the Oilers, had something they wanted to talk over with me. Houston was at that time part of the American Football League, and the AFL was raiding NFL teams mercilessly — much like the emerging World Football League began to do eight years later, in the spring of 1974. It was this feud, between the solidly established NFL and the young, aggressive AFL, that had led to unprecedented six-figure contracts like the ones Namath and a few others had already signed. When Klosterman called I did not yet know that Al Davis, the AFL Commissioner, had escalated this feud into open warfare. Neither did I know that while Davis was hatching a scheme to steal half the NFL's quarterbacks, other men in other offices in the football power structure were trying to head off a crippling price war by arranging a merger between the two rival leagues. I only knew that I couldn't lose anything by listening to what Klosterman had to say because Don was a man I had known and respected for almost ten years. He had been an All-American quarter-back at Loyola, later played in the Canadian League, and had been general manager of pro teams in San Diego and Kansas City. I had always associated him with good, solid situations. Now he was calling from his new office, as general manager of the Houston Oilers.

"John," he said, "we're in a position down here to offer you some cash. We can set things up so that if you want to, all you'll ever have to do is play golf and drink beer and gamble."

I laughed. I enjoyed the sound of that. I was also reminded of stories I'd heard about other players who had signed with Houston in recent years. They would be offered a car a year, or two cars a year, and a ranch somewhere in Texas. Then something would go wrong. The player wouldn't make the team, and the cars and the ranches would all end up in litigation, and the player would be broke. I had heard that one guy signed with the Oilers in exchange for three hundred head of cattle.

But because it was Klosterman I agreed to fly down there for a conversation.

Before he hung up he asked, "Where do you stand with the Forty-niners? How long is your contract?"

"I've got an option clause to play out the coming season," I said, and then added, "I'd love to come down there, but I have to tell you, I'm going to inform the people here of what I'm doing."

Don said that was fine with him, and we set a date.

I went to Lou, told him what was up, and asked him where he planned to be for the next week. He said he was flying up to Portland, if I needed to reach him. I then talked to Bill Johnson, and to Jack Christiansen, the head coach, who didn't much like the sound of it. But

120

about all he could say was, "Well, John, you've got to do what you're going to do. As long as we've discussed it — okay — you'll do what you're going to do."

That night I happened to have dinner with a close friend of mine, Melville "Sonny" Marx, a securities broker and partner in the San Francisco firm of J. Barth and Company. Sonny and I had a lot in common. We both liked golf, and horse racing, and games of every sort. I had first met him in 1961, when Matt Hazeltine and I entered a fund-raising event the San Francisco *Chronicle* sponsored called The World Championship Domino Tournament. Sonny was about fifty-five, an experienced businessman whose opinion I trusted and whose integrity I admired.

Now I didn't have a business manager in those days, which relates to one of the reasons I was interested in Houston. I needed more money than I already had. I'd never been able to save much or invest it wisely. I was thirty-one and starting to feel the need to do something sensible and financially sound. You can't play football forever. I told Sonny that if anything came of this I did not want to be in Houston alone. I asked him if he would come along.

"We can get in a lot of golf down there," I offered. "Three days of golf, on the Oilers."

"I'll tell you what," he said. "I have a horse running at Hollywood Park. If you'll fly to the track with me, we'll root my horse in, and we'll fly on to Houston from Los Angeles."

That's how it worked out. Sonny came along, purely as a friend, and as a kind of counselor, and I was thankful he did. There was no way I could have been prepared for what Don and Bud Adams had to say.

Soon after we checked into the Warwick Hotel, they came up to our room. Don was about thirty-five then, his broad freckled face grinning eagerly. Adams was a little older, a little taller, a good deal rounder. He is a Texas oil man who bought himself a football franchise when the AFL first organized in 1960. He wore leather boots, a string tie, a cowboy hat. It didn't take him long to get to the point. The American Football League was willing to pay me $500,000 to play quarterback with the Houston Oilers for three years.

I seemed to be very cool, hearing this offer, because it wasn't real to me. The figure was so preposterous at first, it just didn't mean anything. Half a million dollars! This put Joe Namath in the shade, and every other athlete I had ever heard of on any playing field in the world.

I sat there trying to look cool. Sonny *was* cool. He told Bud I should be getting at least a million. Bud was surprised by this, but not too disturbed. They started to bargain. Bud had ideas for various kinds of fringe benefits: a Dodge dealership in the Houston area, immediate entry into a high-class country club. They finally settled on a compromise figure of $750,000 dollars, and Sonny said, "Let's see how that looks on paper."

A cocktail napkin was lying on the table. Adams scribbled on it, *The AFL agrees to pay John Brodie $250,000 a season for three seasons.* We all signed the napkin and agreed that was sufficient for the time being.

Realizing my next step was to get in touch with the 49ers, I said, "I don't want to play games with anybody, and start some kind of a bidding war. But I have to give them a chance to match this offer."

Adams said he wouldn't advise waiting too long to close the thing. So with him and Klosterman and Sonny Marx listening in, I called Lou Spadia in Portland, where he had gone to attend his son's graduation from college.

He was hit between the eyes. "Christ, John! I can't believe that!"

I understood his feeling. I still couldn't believe it myself. I said, "Lou, I have signed this agreement, subject to your meeting it. I'm obligated not to settle for less because it wouldn't be fair to these guys who are making me this offer. And it wouldn't be fair to me because it's too much money to turn down. You don't have to top it, Lou. If you can match it, I'll stay with San Francisco."

Lou still couldn't believe it. He told me to sit tight, and he would send Jack White, the general manager, down there to check this out. I said, "Okay, we'll wait, Lou. But these guys want a decision within eight hours."

Jack White caught the next plane out of San Francisco, flew into Houston, raced to the Warwick by cab, studied the napkin, and verified all the terms with Adams and Klosterman. Then he called Lou in Portland.

"It's true, Lou, it's accurate, and they are ready to do it."

Lou, who by this time had sat through his son's graduation in such a distracted state he had missed most of the ceremony, told us all once again to sit tight. I knew he was stalling, and I regretted having to put him in such a bind. I could see no way he was going to match that kind of money. The eight-hour deadline passed, with no more word from the West Coast. I figured that was the end of it. I went to sleep assuming I had signed with the Houston Oilers for three quarters of a million.

Next morning Adams and Klosterman were back up in our hotel room. I said it was nice to be seeing my new employers this early in the day. Don's natural enthusiasm had dimmed. He smiled tentatively and said, yes, it was good to see us too and although a couple of problems had come up, we would be able to handle those and then everything would indeed be fine. I said, "What kind of problems?"

Bud Adams suggested that he and I step into the adjoining room. I remember saying, "There's nothing I have to hide, and if there is nothing you have to hide, why don't we just throw it all out here where we can all look at it?" But Bud was insistent, so Sonny said I'd better go along with him and see what Bud had on his mind.

I brought my putter and a golf ball with me into the bedroom. I had been looking forward to playing a lot of golf in Houston; so had Sonny. Now we found ourselves trapped inside the hotel. Bud and Don were adamant that we "not be seen anywhere around town." By that morning I was getting restless. I felt like practicing my putts. While Bud warmed to his topic I started knocking short ones up against the bedroom wall.

"John," he said at last, "do you think you would possibly be interested in a full-time Dodge dealership here in Houston?"

I missed my golf ball completely. I looked over at him. "What in the hell are you talking about?"

"Since last night a couple of things have come up, John, and it may be that you'll be back in San Francisco after all. But I know we can work out the arrangements to be satisfactory to everybody . . ."

I said, "Whoa there, Bud. I don't want to talk about any Dodge dealership. I can hardly drive a car, let alone sell one. I'm a ballplayer. I came down here to talk about playing football."

124

He kept on about this Dodge dealership as if it were already a fact of life, while I kept thinking about those other players I'd heard of who had come to Houston expecting ranches and cattle herds. I put my putter down and said we ought to go back out into the other room.

Don and Sonny were sitting there looking at each other. I asked Don what was going on. He and Bud muttered and cleared their throats and finally Don said their hands were tied.

I said, "Look. I signed an agreement with you guys, which has already created a certain loss of affinity with my former employer. I don't much care to fly back tomorrow and say, 'Hey, I made a little mistake, but that's all cleared up now, and here I am.' "

Don said something to the effect that Bud had been up all night getting calls from other owners and that in the last twelve hours everything had changed. "The leagues are getting ready to merge," he said. "It's happening a lot sooner than we thought. If we sign you now, it will foul up the merger."

"But didn't we make a deal?" I asked.

Don said we did.

"And we all signed that cocktail napkin?"

He said we had, but he just couldn't say much more about it at the moment.

"Well, let me ask you this," I said. "If it gets down to the nut cutting, you'll say what happened, right?"

"Right."

He knew that I knew that, and that I knew he was in a tight squeeze himself; and I trusted him to fill me in sooner or later.

Meanwhile Adams had started talking to Sonny about

125

the make-up of football players, how you might reach an agreement with one of them but you know how they will rescind a contract and not fulfill their obligations, and thus when you're dealing with players it's a special kind of business; contracts are made and broken all the time in the football world, and this has become an acceptable kind of procedure.

Sonny said, "Well, in my business it's not an acceptable procedure, and I don't think it's acceptable to John, or he would have taken you up on this dealership."

"As far as I'm concerned," I said, "we have an agreement. I couldn't go back on my word, and I wouldn't expect you to go back on yours."

Adams said, "All right. I am a man of my word. Don't worry. We'll be getting back to you."

That's where it stood when they left the hotel room, saying they'd be getting back to us. As soon as the door was shut, Sonny said, "Pack your goddamn bag." He was ready to leave anyway. Hiding out in the hotel was costing him money; he had already lost thirty-two dollars in domino games. We flew out of Houston that afternoon.

About a week later the AFL and the NFL announced that they had merged. A reporter called me to ask what I thought of this. I told him that as far as I was concerned I had signed a binding agreement with the American Football League and where it went from there was their problem.

"Their problem" was a large one. The fact that the offer had come from the league, rather than from the Houston team itself, was at the center of it. Al Davis had taken over as commissioner of the AFL just that April, and immediately he put together a war chest of a few million dollars with the specific goal of strengthening the AFL and weakening the NFL by seducing away as many of its top players as possible, especially the quarterbacks. I found out later that several other men besides myself had been ready to sign when the red flag went up. The crazy thing was — and this just indicates how divided the feeling was among the men who controlled the football business — serious merger talk among various owners had begun just about the time Al Davis took over the league and started his raiding campaign.

It has been said that the offer made to me somehow forced the merger. This isn't really true. It was typical of what was forcing the leagues together. But mainly it was a matter of lucky timing. Lucky for me. While I was down there in the Warwick Hotel, all the merger talk was coming to a head; other men in other cities were talking just as fast, trying to reach an agreement before the talent war got entirely out of control.

The merger announcement ended that war, which meant all the quarterbacks who'd been ready to defect were expected to go back to their teams and forget it. Somehow the other players who had been approached were either paid off, or kept quiet, or ignored. My case was the only one to gain wide attention. I believe there were two reasons for this. First, the timing. Two or three days more, and there wouldn't have been an offer. Second, the openness of the conversation. If I had gone to Houston myself, if I had dealt secretly with Adams, his offer might never have left that hotel room. As it turned out, we had nothing *but* the talk to base our claim on. There was no material evidence. The cocktail napkin we signed never left Houston. It never left the Warwick Hotel. I lost it. "Man, ain't you a dilly!" Sonny chided. He almost hit me with his suitcase. But he had heard the offer. The 49ers management had heard and seen the terms. I give credit to Don and Bud Adams, they never hedged. They honored the whole deal. To this day I don't know if they were aware that the napkin itself had disappeared, but it seemed like a good idea to keep quiet on that subject at the time.

Back in California, I consulted with my brother, Bill, a lawyer in Palo Alto. He too had flown to Houston, soon after Jack White did, to observe the proceedings. Sonny suggested to Bill and I that we might do well to get in touch with John Elliott "Doc" Cook, the ablest attorney he knew and a specialist in corporate and antitrust law. Doc was about sixty-seven then and supposedly retired but still a very active man. He agreed to listen to the details. We tape-recorded everything that had happened. Doc asked me if I thought my position was clean. I said I thought it was. He then said if we wanted him to be involved, he would do whatever he could to assist us. And that's the way it developed; from then on he and Bill worked together. Doc took the position that it wasn't fair to make an offer like that to a player and then have it nullified by a high-level power struggle. He agreed to handle my case — Brodie versus The Whole Football Establishment — and his first demand was for a million dollars plus legal fees.

This was in June. Training camp would be starting in not too many weeks. I assumed then that I'd be back with the 49ers for the '67 season. Doc said not to assume anything. He advised me to say nothing to anyone and in fact suggested it would be an excellent idea if I just took my family and disappeared for a while, got away from the football scene entirely. So I took Sue and our four kids over to the windward side of Oahu. We had a beach cottage there overlooking a lagoon. It was so remote and out of the way that the only people who found us were Don Klosterman, Y. A. Tittle, and a photographer from *Sports Illustrated*, which ran a full-page picture of us in hiding.

Don flew over to find out where I stood personally in the matter. I made clear to him what he really knew ahead of time: I had put everything into Doc Cook's hands and was letting him handle it now. Don came representing, not the Oilers, and not the AFL, but both leagues. Having merged, they now shared the common problem of Doc Cook's demand. It included the threat of an antitrust suit, which was something the leagues could not afford just then, financially or legally. Financially it could treble the damages. Legally, the very existence of such a suit might hold up government approval of their merger.

Meanwhile YAT chased me down and put a call through from the mainland. His first concern was whether or not all this was going to affect my football game. If anyone understood how you can get mangled in the machinery it was YAT. "John," he said, "I don't know all the specifics of this deal, but when it gets straightened out, get your ass back here. Don't let those people end up screwing you because of their conflicts and power battles."

I appreciated that kind of support. I needed it. Everyone else was looking at the money. But I was also thinking about the team and about the start of training camp.

129

After all the smoke cleared, I was still going to be a quarterback, and it was that time of year when you start getting in shape for the new season, a habit not easily broken once you get into it. The pro ballplayer's year divides into its own special cycle: spring, you bargain; late summer, you train; fall, you have a go at it; winter, you recuperate. I wanted to settle this matter. At the same time, something inside me yearned to fly back to California for the opening of camp. Doc Cook told me to sit tight a while longer, that a settlement was near. So I did. But I was getting tired of sitting tight. I didn't like it. I'd had enough legal strategy. I was squirming to play football.

Early in August, Doc, and Lou Spadia, and Pete Rozelle, commissioner of the merged leagues, reached an agreement I was glad to accept. Doc said the leagues' liability was such that I could get even more if I waited a while longer, perhaps a month or two. I didn't want to wait another month or two. I didn't want to miss another day of training camp. I had already missed two weeks. I was feeling guilty lolling around the beach in Hawaii. I genuinely wanted to be back with the team. Why hold out for more when the settlement gave me what I felt I was due at that point — that is, what the AFL had agreed to in May. Part of it would be paid during the next three seasons and the rest after I finished playing football. It would come to me through the 49ers office, but everyone knew a good portion was being coughed up by all the other clubs in both leagues. During the next couple of years I heard more than one owner complain about having to pay money to the quarterback his team was supposed to be trying to beat. I didn't worry about that too much. I figured it was an owner's problem, not a player's problem. Hadn't they brought it on themselves?

130

Together with legal fees the total came to $910,000. I've been told that this deal set a record, that at the time it was the largest amount of money ever offered to a professional athlete. The most significant part of the whole episode, for me, was not the amount, nor was it the mechanics of the deal — the who-got-strong-armed-into-paying-what-to-whom; it was the effects this soon began to have upon the rest of my life.

It can weigh you down, being billed as THE MILLION DOLLAR QUARTERBACK, when you're still trying to play a good game of football every Sunday. Lou Spadia said later I was one of the few athletes he has known who signed a jumbo contract and survived it with his life intact. Intact, yes. But not unscathed.

Lines of
Communication

12 ALL THE EFFORT I had put into
success on the ball field seemed to be paying off. Else-
where, nothing much had changed. I was soon to discover that the thing I had learned to do so well in the
huddle — communicate — was exactly what I was failing
to do at all well in my personal life. There were several
skills like that, which I had developed to play the game
yet had neglected off the field — planning ahead, responsibility to others, etc., etc.

It's often said that football players are boys who haven't
grown up yet. I guess I started growing up around 1966.
I'd had blinders on all my life. You talk about tunnel
vision. If it didn't have a ball, or a mitt, or a racket, or a
club, it didn't hold my interest. This attitude started to
catch up with me, ironically, just about the time I signed
the big contract. Sue and I were going through a pretty
rough time in our marriage. We just weren't getting
along. The problem clearly was not outside. It was inside. It was in the spring of 1966 that for the first time I
felt a powerful need to look inside myself, to somehow

132

get far enough outside my own self-preoccupation to see what was really going on inside.

I didn't know where to start. I just felt the need. I was looking for answers before I even knew what the questions were. Some friends told us about a seminar down in Monterey, a kind of encounter group, which sounded interesting. Sue and I had never been involved in anything like that. It wasn't the sort of thing football players bothered with. But we decided to try it. We had to start somewhere. If we hadn't tried this seminar we would have stumbled into another one with a similar goal — which was basically to start people understanding themselves a little better. Programs were popping up all over California.

What I remember most vividly is an experiment with a T-square, a big puzzle in the shape of a T. It was an exercise in communication. Sue and I were seated back to back. I was given the completed puzzle, she was given the unassembled pieces of the same puzzle, and I was supposed to guide her in putting it together. Neither of us could see what the other was doing. We could only talk. Everyone in the group had been asked to go through this, and no two people had been able to get the puzzle assembled. It was comical. We had watched men end up yelling at each other, "Well listen, you stupid sonofabitch! Just take that goddamn piece and put it *there!*" And the other guy would say, "Well, screw you, I can't even understand what you're talking about!"

After watching this a few times I couldn't wait to try my hand at it. I knew damn well I could get Sue to put those pieces together in record time. It just looked like the simplest thing in the world. When our turn came we sat down facing in opposite directions, and I began to describe the layout. "Take the long one with the sort of squared-off edge," I would say, "and put it up next to the other long piece . . ." And Sue tried to follow these instructions.

When the leader told us time was up, I turned around hopefully. "Well, let's see what ya got." It was the worst-looking jumble I could imagine, much worse than it would have been if no one had said anything to Sue. We looked at that, and we couldn't do anything but laugh. It reminded me of the time I got kicked out of the ROTC at the end of my sophomore year at Stanford. I was a cadet corporal, demonstrating how well I could drill a platoon. It was a formal parade at the polo field, with spectators in the stands and the prestige of the unit at stake. It took me about five minutes of barking out the drill commands to get sixteen men spread all over the field and heading in four directions at once. Finally I just had to call out, "Hey, you guys, everybody just come on back here and regroup."

It was that kind of signal-crossing Sue and I were laughing at as we looked at the confusion of T-square pieces. Then we looked up at each other and got the message loud and clear: this could be an image of where we had been in our relationship for years.

That was actually an exercise in noncommunication. It exposed a weakness but didn't go much farther. What I gained was a lot of awareness about what I did *not* know, which in some ways left me worse off than before.

But this one weekend also opened my eyes to several things: the need for better communication, my own general lack of awareness, and the need for a shift in my relationships with other people. Until then I had been too

134

much preoccupied with appearances, with how I looked in public, what I wore, the kind of attention I could draw to myself, the stories I could tell in a bar or around a dinner table, and with being one of the guys. These things were of supreme importance to me. I aspired to be what I thought was an *interesting* person. After that seminar, although I had a long way to go, I began to see the value of being an *interested* person. It was a step.

When I reported back to 49er headquarters in August I found that communication lines were snarled in another area. I wanted to sit at a table with Lou and Jack Christiansen and make sure we were all in accord on what had happened and how we would proceed from here. But I never could get all three of us into the same room at the same time. Jack did not like what had happened. He resented it. He felt I had held out on the team, had broken faith with the team, or something like that. The first thing he did was fine me three thousand dollars for getting back late to training camp. And I resented *that*. I paid it. But I felt it was an unjustified punishment for something that was really being handled at a much higher level than coach-player.

Jack and I had known each other a long time. He had been an assistant coach since 1959 (coming to the 49ers from Detroit, where he'd been an All-Pro defensive back). Even after he became head coach we still socialized for a while, went out drinking from time to time. And nowadays — now that we are both long gone from the 49ers — we get along fine again. But for two seasons there — '66 and '67 — he and I drew farther and farthar apart.

It is hard enough for head coaches and quarterbacks to

135

stay friendly in the pros. For some reason, player-coach relationships generally are almost always at a distance. The coaches often have a fear of taking a player into confidence and then sending him back to the group. This basic gap is not simply going to stay fixed. It is either going to close up or get wider, which is why it often grows into a very wide gap. I would say that the relationship between head coaches and quarterbacks is the most difficult in professional football. They both have a lot of responsibility for what happens on the field. As long as they agree on who is in control of what, everything is okay. But a coach who is not quite sure of his ability to control the whole operation of a team can very easily get threatened by the degree of control that naturally falls to a quarterback who is doing his full job at that position. Somewhere in his heart of hearts every coach wants to be a quarterback, and it is hard to find a quarterback who doesn't think he is smarter — in his own area — than the coach, especially if he's a veteran with eight or ten years' experience. Your favorite teammate could move up into the head coach slot, and it would be a miracle if you remained good friends while he held the job. It has been said that a quarterback doesn't really come of age until he can tell his coach to go fly a kite. Well, by that definition I had come of age long before 1966. And this misunderstanding over the origins of my jumbo payment did not help matters much at all.

The players, on the other hand, saw things a little differently. One morning soon after I got back from Hawaii, I had breakfast with Bernie Casey. I remember him telling me, "I haven't heard one guy say anything negative, John. Their attitude is, let him do whatever he has to do and then come on back and play football."

Far from being threatened, or resenting me, other players saw this settlement as another portent of good things to come for a lot of players. The older guys on the team in particular were smart enough to see that all the salaries were likely to be going up. It wasn't long before I was hearing from men on other teams, quarterbacks, wanting to know the details of what had happened, how much was I really making and how the deal had been put together. This kind of player-to-player consultation was something that had not happened much up to that time. The Players Association, although it had existed since 1956, was still rather loosely organized. Members of the same team were encouraged by management not to discuss contract terms. Players from different teams seldom compared notes. I shared what I knew with Sonny Jurgensen and Roman Gabriel and several others who contacted me. John Unitas, who has been a good friend of mine over the years, asked to see the contract, so I sent him a copy. All this had its effect on the inevitable increase in salaries. If the owners had hoped to stem the tide of high contracts, they figured wrong.

My first day back I suited up and reported for practice. When I hunched down over Bruce Bosley, the center, what he handed up to me felt strange for a football. It was a little small and was covered with prickles. It was sticky too. He had smuggled a Hawaiian pineapple up to the scrimmage line, with a note pinned to it: ONE MIL-LION DOLLARS, MINUS THREE THOUSAND.

That was the general attitude of the guys on the team. We all had a good laugh. For a while it seemed as if, in spite of all the publicity, things were back to normal. I would get back into shape, and we would move on from where we had been at the end of last season.

137

But they weren't back to normal. There was no such thing as "normal." Something always comes along to stir up the stew. For one thing, Jack was starting to groom young George Mira, who had been chomping at his bit since 1964, unsatisfied to be the back-up man, aching and anxious to have a team of his own. Jack never did entirely approve of the way I played quarterback. At Detroit he had played with Bobby Layne, and he admired Layne tremendously for the way he could beat a defense. Now nobody has more respect for Bobby Layne than I do, but he and I played a whole lot differently. When things were going along all right, Jack would allow me my style. But if something started to go wrong, if we lost a couple of games, then the sparks would start to fly between me and Jack. And Mira, he wouldn't even stop to listen; he was pulling his helmet on and heading for the field.

Meanwhile the fans had decided that any quarterback getting paid a million dollars should be putting on a million-dollar show every week, and if he wasn't, then he'd be better off turning in his pads. The press was partly responsible for this; they just couldn't leave my case alone. It was too juicy. The local reporters had a hard time at first getting the whole story straight. Gossip ran rampant. Every time a new detail or rumor was uncovered, there would be another round of columns on the subject. It was so much money that it couldn't be ignored. Most people want a lot of money but often have trouble watching someone else making it. Some love him, and some hate him for it. I got caught in the middle there, between the love and the hate. This is finally what started to affect my playing. Not the money itself, and my own relationship to it, but the way others related to the money and thus what they began to direct at me and expect of me.

If it happened today, I would be able to handle it without much difficulty. At the time I began to feel very uncomfortable every time the money was mentioned. A fan or a reporter would want to know, "How come a goddamn football player is paid so much?" And my reaction was, "Dammit, why can't we just forget that and talk about the football game."

I felt resentment coming at me from all sides. And I fought it. If I had been a little wiser, I would have understood where it was coming from and gone on out there and simply played the best football I could. But internally I fought the resentment, and this began to show in my playing, which in turn sometimes led to even stronger reactions from the fans. Mira was their boy, much as I had been when Tittle was the aging but still first-string quarterback, and as Tittle had been before he replaced Frank Albert. Mira was "the winner" now; I had become the goat.

I remember a game against Green Bay in which George played the whole game. We were ahead 21-20 when he threw an interception and got hurt on the same play. Because it was an interception, George came right off the field. Because he was injured, when we got the ball back, I ran out to take over. The fans didn't know George had been injured. They thought he had been replaced for throwing that one interception after playing a fine game all afternoon. They were full of rage. They built up such a fury of booing when they saw me trotting onto the field that by the time we got to the line of scrimmage, we couldn't get the play off. No one could hear the signals.

It was like the Roman Colosseum filled with 60,000 people all clamoring for slaughter. John David Crow turned and gave the whole crowd the finger and screamed out a string of obscenities. We actually got so fired up by his defiance that we moved the ball eighty yards.

For the team 1966 was a fifty-fifty year. We won six, we lost six, we tied two. For me, it was a respectable year. I completed 232 passes, I broke some 49er records. The last half of the season I felt I played five very good games. It was one of those seasons when I knew my own performance was solid, even though few people gave me credit for it. This knowledge in itself helped me weather the stress I was living with. This was the year I really began to understand what Tittle had been going through in the late fifties. The sequence was exactly the same. At the age of thirty-one, after ten years of pro ball, and after his most successful season, he had begun to fall from grace. Now — partly *because* of my success — the feeling on the coaching staff was to look with ever more favor on George Mira. My awareness of this became another negative factor affecting my play.

By the time the '67 season started I had two of these young bucks to contend with. The 49ers hired Steve Spurrier, All-American quarterback and Heisman Trophy winner from the University of Florida, a deceptively easygoing guy who looked like somebody's kid brother and could punt like Jim Thorpe. The 49ers had more quarterback talent lined up than any other team in the country. It meant double pressure for me. By the end of that season Jack Christiansen was talking about "the George Mira Era." I felt like some kind of dinosaur that would soon become extinct.

140

The trouble was, I'd usually hear statements like this first by reading them in the papers. Remembering what had happened to Tittle and how he bore so much of his burden in silence, I was at least going to try and get the news face to face. I couldn't take my case to the papers, after all; published complaints from quarterbacks always sound like bellyaching and self-pity (and generally they are). In fact, there is almost no way a playing quarterback can get a public hearing for his case without coming off like a crybaby. I would try to sit down and talk about these stories in the paper, but for some reason opinions would appear in print that we never could quite discuss in private. That's how bad communication had become between me and the coaching staff. It was a classic example of something that happens all too often in football. When there is a problem in communication, the egos jump right out into the foreground and the problem just gets worse. You don't solve it; you merely stop communicating.

Even with Tittle, who was one guy there who understood my predicament and stood up for me all throughout this period, even with Y.A. things were not quite right. You might say he and I still had one more battle to fight, and it happened — almost — one day on the practice field in Redwood City. It was a tense time for everyone. We had come through the first half of the season with a 5-1 record. Then things began to fall apart, and no one could agree on why. I was blaming certain changes in the offensive system. Chris was blaming me. Y.A. was defending me. From week to week no one knew who was going to start at quarterback or who was going to start as receivers. The coaches were all worried about their jobs.

Since Tittle was on my side it may seem strange that

our old feud should come boiling up to the surface at this particular time. To explain it I have to explain something about his methods as a coach. I have said he was a theorist. He was a brilliant theorist. If he had any short-comings as a coach, it was in the way he delivered his theories, which would be in the form of long, carefully worked out speeches — monologues — during which he couldn't stand to be interrupted. He might take half an hour to explain a point from every side of the fence, then he'd ask a question and before anyone could answer it, he would provide his own answer. The man was thorough. And he was enjoyable to listen to because he'd bolster his points with east Texas anecdotes. During a season he might repeat some of these monologues several times, usually with good reason, because someone had not got it clear the first time. He was always willing to go through it again. My problem was that he and I had talked through all the theory so many ways I knew his speeches from top to bottom. I would get impatient. Hearing one coming, I would needle him. We might be sitting in a meeting for offensive backs and receivers, and he would be at the blackboard winding up to go over something again in order to make sure there was no misunder-standing and I would say, "God*damn,* Y! I think we got that one the fifth time through."

He would start to steam. "How do you know what I'm going to say? Well . . . maybe you *do* know. But I'm going over it again, and it takes me a while to get my point across. But I know what I'm thinking and you don't necessarily know. So just sit your ass down and listen to the whole damn thing."

So I would sit there and heckle him silently, making

142

faces, rolling my eyes, punching my cheek out with my tongue like a high school kid trying to get a rise out of his teacher.

I finally succeeded the afternoon Y.A. started to bait me on the practice field. It was more than the heckling that pushed him to it. It was that insult in the locker room in 1963. It was the time I aced him out of the squad scrimmage in 1958. Moments like those still lived inside him somewhere, bits and pieces of them that still had to be cleaned out. It was all the pressure of the whole team in 1967 too. My game was not as sharp as it had been. Tittle knew why, but he wanted me to be doing better in spite of it. He was feeling sort of fatherly about me. He knew what was going on with me. He knew from his own experience how it ought to be handled, and he had filled up with a kind of frustrated anger, the way a father can when his son doesn't live up to some expectation.

It was a Tuesday, our first practice after a loss on Sunday. Early in the afternoon we watched the game films. I knew, as I relived each series, that I had played badly, and I knew why. When the films were over, Tittle wanted to talk about my game. He had already discussed it with the staff, now he wanted to discuss it with me. One of the problems was that I had failed to do something we had agreed on, during pregame planning, to strengthen the attack. It had to do with throwing more balls to the backs. But that was not really the issue. The issue was the way I reacted when he raised this point.

I offered some justification for my play, which he didn't accept. He thought he could help me if we tried to analyze what had gone wrong. I could hear one of his theories coming, a little monologue I was in no mood to

143

listen to. I was short with him. I said, "Goddamn it, Y, let's cut the bullshit, okay? I don't really want to get into all this philosophy."

He didn't say another word. He clamped his jaws shut and walked away. He let this fester inside him for an hour and a half, until he couldn't hold it any longer. We were out on the field running plays, just the offensive team, without pads. Y.A. was standing about seven feet behind the huddle, and he started whispering at me.

"You asshole, Brodie. Why don't you come on over here?"

I tried to ignore it. I was already regretting what I had said to him. I called some more plays. He wouldn't let up. "Brodie, you chickenshit sonofabitch. C'mon. C'mon over here. I'm going to kick your butt once and for all."

Finally I'd had it. I straightened up from the huddle and yelled, "Goddamn it, Tittle, get off my ass!"

He said, "You can't make me."

I went for him, and swung, aiming for his jaw. I really did want to deck him. He ducked, and came up swinging, and we would have been into it, but before he could land a clear punch, two guys grabbed him from behind. Two other guys grabbed me, and the whole team and all the coaches were ganged around looking at us, sort of embarrassed and perplexed.

For the next day and a half Y.A. was livid and would not speak to me. And I wasn't in much of a mood to talk to him, although the more time that passed the funnier it all seemed to me. By game time that weekend I'm sure we both figured some kind of truce had to be arranged since he was upstairs on the phones. When the other team had

144

the ball he and I were supposed to be conferring about strategy. Before the game I said, "Tittle, we don't have to like each other too much, but I think it would be a good idea if we talked a few things over." He said, yeah, he thought it might be a good idea. So we talked and during the next two days we got it cleared up, got our near fight cleared up, and also all the bad feeling that had flowed between us for the past ten years. It took that long — from 1957 to 1967 — during which time Y.A. had been my opponent, my rival, my teacher and coach, then briefly my opponent again. Ever since, we have been close friends. His home is a few miles from mine, down the Peninsula south of San Francisco. He has his insurance office in the same building where my brother practices law. We are both retired quarterbacks now and can laugh together about all the trouble we gave each other.

The funny thing is, that struggle was coming to its ridiculous conclusion while I was deep into the early stages of my own struggle for survival with the young quarterback trying to unseat me. It was getting bad. It was starting to overwhelm me. The very fact that I could take a swing at any coach is a pretty good indication of how edgy I was, how close to the surface my hostility was.

It showed again one afternoon when the team was loping onto the field for a home game at Kezar. I had been getting booed with furious glee, booed like never before, and I had reached a point where I had absolutely had it with all criticism, especially from the fans. This was the year, by the way, when the stadium officials had to build a screen over the exposed section of the players' tunnel to protect us from unidentified flying objects. On this par-

145

ticular afternoon it seemed as if they had been waiting for me to make my appearance, as if they had been saving their wind all week to deliver the mightiest boo of the decade. When I ran out of the tunnel and into the stadium, the booing and bellowing rolled down over me. As I reached the grass I turned toward the stands and gave all forty thousand spectators the Russian salute. I slapped my bicep and shoved my fist and one extended finger into the air and waved it to all sides of the stadium.

My attitude went something like this: "Okay, you bastards, we're not going to discuss it in the papers. This is strictly between you and me. I'm out here doing as well as I can. I am not quitting because you think I'm doing a bad job. I really don't believe that. So here I am, like it or not. I have been elected to play, and if you guys think you can do better you are entitled to try out for the job. Otherwise shut up and let's get on with the game."

While I jogged on out to warm up, the noise around me doubled. The booers — who now made up what seemed like half the crowd — booed with new commitment. The other half were cheering. They liked this show. I felt a little better after that. I had got my message across. They had a better idea now of how I felt about it. Maybe this even mellowed some of the booers for a while. But I am not proud of what I did that afternoon. It was a hate message. At that moment I despised them all.

My skin was so thin that season even opposing linemen were getting through to me, even Alex Karras, the great Detroit pass rusher who I knew from long experience was a sharp and devious heckler. Certain players will try anything they can think of to ruffle and rattle the quarterback. They will scowl, they will threaten, they will mock and

146

badger you. I had long since learned that the wisest pol-
icy was not to give them any satisfaction. A player has
the right, on the field, to do anything he can to gain an advantage; and I have the right to ignore him. The day we
played Detroit, Karras hit me twice in a row, with all his
force and speed, and each time we got up he said, with
this mocking edge to his voice, "It's going to be a rough
afternoon, kid." The third time he did this I couldn't ignore it. I wasn't cool. I was frustrated at the way this
game was going — they were ahead 21-3 and ended up
beating us 45-3 — I was frustrated at the way the season
was going. I was out of control. He hit me again and
said, "I told you, kid, it's going to be a rough afternoon."
And I blurted something brilliant like, "Well, fuck you,
you big prick!" He lumbered away, pleased with himself. On the next play he hit me again, and this time as he
got up he lisped, "Ooh, did her hurt her pussy?" That really pissed me off. I blurted something else that showed
how touchy I was, and Karras walked away smirking. He
knew he had me. He knew he'd done more damage to
my game that day than ten of his crunching tackles ever
could.

You can't play very good football when you're hating
the fans, and not communicating with the coaches, and
uptight about the young quarterback who's gunning for
your job, and letting the defensive linemen call your
bluff. By the middle of the season I was right where YAT
had been during my second year with the team; I was an
All-Pro quarterback, with the highest contract in the history of athletics, sitting on the bench.

GETTING HIT

THERE ARE A lot of reasons not to like football. One of them, for the player, is being overwhelmed by it, as I almost was in 1967. Another is the so-called violence of the game. Some people criticize this game because men hurl themselves at one another and some of them get hurt and blood comes spilling down the jersey. Well, there are various kinds of violence, and not all of them are bad. For one thing, what you see in professional football is voluntary violence. Nobody gets hurt but the men who play it, and they have taken a good look at what they're doing and they go into the game knowing its risks.

The people who watch it are doing so voluntarily too. Everybody has the option not to watch it. If enough people elected not to watch football, there wouldn't be a game. Imagine twenty-two guys out there in an empty stadium, all suited up and doing all those things to each other with absolutely nobody watching. It would never happen. They need the fans, and the fans need the ballplayers, and somehow the game would lose a bit if we were playing two-hands-below-the-waist.

148

I'm not saying anybody *likes* to get his butt knocked off play after play after play. But there is something about the physical impact that tests a man in a certain way, challenges him. If you don't have a taste for that kind of challenge, you take up another line of work.

I'm speaking as a quarterback, of course, which means I see the violence of the game a whole lot differently than a linebacker or tackle does. The tackle's main job is physically hitting his man and moving him out of the play. Once the play is called, my main job is getting the ball into motion before somebody hits me and throws me for a loss. In order to do that effectively, there's a lot of action I just have to take for granted. I mean, I *know* that all those guys in the defensive line are 6-5 and weigh 270 and can run the hundred in 10.1. I know they'll do anything they can think of to cow me or spoil my game. And I know I'm going to get hit hard by one or two or three of them several times a game. I just put all that out of my mind. If a quarterback's mind is on the rush, there is no way he can execute the play. So the hitting was always second nature to me. All my attention had to be downfield. By the time Karras had planted me in the grass — if I was cool enough to ignore his taunts — my mind would already be on the next call.

I have never bought the old adage, by the way, that a quarterback must step forward when he throws. He doesn't really need to step that much. I always preferred to drop back and stay planted. Then I could throw it anywhere — outside, inside, down the field. Once you move forward, you cut down your ability to throw to the sideline; and linebackers all know that. If you get hit while moving forward, the ball is more likely to go up in

149

the air than anywhere else. If you're standing there and receive a blow, you can still make a motion over the top of the tackler, or through him, or around him. A quarterback is better off catching a blow than moving into a blow. What's necessary is to shift your weight over the top of your body so that, even if hit while throwing, your upper body is thrust forward and can still finish the motion. I always figured they could have the rest of it.

A New Era,
an Old Wound

13 THE WAY THINGS STOOD I knew I couldn't keep playing for the 49ers. If the team was going to get anywhere, and if I was going to get anywhere, something had to change. I was the first to admit that I had been part of the problem. George Mira played the last two games of the '67 season, and the team won them both. A lot of people were saying that my act was over for good. Most of the guys on the team figured, one way or another, I'd be gone by next season. Even my father was advising me to leave, to go looking for another team, a better team. He always took a lot of pride in my playing. He loved to sit around and talk about football with his cronies. You can imagine how hard it must have been listening to all that booing aimed down at his son. He genuinely felt that 1967 *had* to be my last year in San Francisco.

I wasn't arguing with him, or with any of the trading rumors that were circulating during those months. The chemistry had gone wrong again. Communication lines were down. I felt totally undone by a situation that was out of my control — partly my own fault, partly the

151

coaches' policies, partly the crazy sequence of events that had left me with the blessing and the curse of a small fortune. Someone wiser might have been content to take the money and run. Not me. People often laugh when a ballplayer says he really isn't in it for the money. Well, of course, you want to get paid for playing, and you'd rather make more than less. But I'll say it again: money was never my main motive. I still wanted to play football — if I could find the right combination. And I still wanted that one thing I had never yet had in pro ball: a title-winning team.

The chemistry began to change when Dick Nolan showed up. He was brought in to take over as head coach. Nolan had played nine years as a defensive back with the Giants, the Chicago Cardinals, and finally with the Dallas Cowboys, where he had coached for six years before coming to San Francisco. I didn't know Dick. I had only played against him once, way back in that 1957 All-Star Game. On the day he first asked me to come into his office, I didn't know where he stood in his thinking about the team, or about me, and I didn't much care. All I really wanted from this interview was a chance to explain why I wanted out. I wanted my intentions to be clear so there would be no misunderstanding.

Nolan has a craggy face. It could be a prize fighter's face. He has a tough veneer and appears to be much harder than he is, especially when you first meet him. I learned later that he was as tough as any man I've ever known when it came to effort expended. If you could measure success by time invested in getting a job done, Dick would be at the top of the list. He drove himself relentlessly.

When I first walked into his office that day he seemed unnecessarily gruff, short, remote. It put me a little off balance.

He was talking to an assistant coach. Without looking up or saying hello, he said, "I'll be with you in a minute," which sounded to me like *I'll get to you when I call for you.*

I wasn't in a very charitable mood to begin with. This pissed me off. His next line didn't improve my outlook. When the assistant coach left, Nolan said, "You want to talk to me?"

Well, I had the impression that he had set this meeting up. I said, "I thought *you* wanted to talk to *me.*"

He nodded and admitted that he did.

"Do you still want to play football here?" he said.

"In the present situation, I really don't."

"I'll be straight with you," he said. "I don't care about all this stuff that has gone on in the past. I know this. I know that in nineteen sixty-five and nineteen sixty-six you were the best quarterback in football. Last year something happened. Your performance wasn't too good. I don't know about all the whys. I have heard a ton of rumors about it, but until I see for myself whether they're true or not, as far as I'm concerned, you'd be starting out fresh."

"What I want to know," I said, "is what's going to happen when we play? Is George going to be playing a lot? Is Spurrier still going to be here? I mean, if I did stick around, how would we figure this thing out? There isn't room to play three quarterbacks."

"You three guys would all start even. At the end of the exhibition season, I'll make a judgment as to who the best

153

guy is, and the one who's most suitable to play for this team, and he will be the guy."

"Is that all there is to it?" I asked. "I don't want to go through any more crap, and I don't want to be made the goat anymore. It's just a simple matter of the best guy gets the job?"

Nolan assured me he would stick to that. And from that conversation on, it was as if my career had indeed started over. This cleaned the slate. I figured I could beat out the two younger quarterbacks. It was up to me to go do it. Very soon my whole outlook began to change. Once again I renewed my enthusiasm for football, with the aim to play it as proficiently as I could.

The difference was that now I realized football could not occupy all of my life. I had made that mistake in 1964. I had gone after the game then with renewed purpose, and I had succeeded in my purpose. I had played better than ever, had received the awards, and had been paid well. Yet I wasn't really any happier. When things started to go wrong, I still didn't have the resources to cope. In fact, when the same things started to go wrong in my personal life, it came down harder on me because I could no longer say that what I needed was more recognition or more money. I knew now that there were other areas of my life I had consistently neglected. The encounter session helped me see that. In 1967 I had also met a few times with a psychologist in San Jose, who counseled me through some of the rougher moments that season. This time, I told myself, I am going to play the game because it is my profession; I'll play it as well as I can, but meanwhile there are other areas I'm going to change. I was going to make things go right on the field and also work at making them go well off the field. And I was going to do this on my own. I did not know quite how. I did not yet realize there was a fully developed system for accomplishing this.

The 49ers organization began to change from top to bottom, and not without some losses I was sorry to see. Bill Johnson moved on to Cincinnati after twenty years with the team as player and as coach. About halfway through the season Tittle quit coaching to devote full time to his insurance business. It was hard to watch those men depart, but there was reason to be hopeful about Nolan's arrival. He saw that his first priority was to shore up the defensive team, which had for years been the 49ers' main weakness. From my own point of view, if we had a defense to match our offense, maybe fewer analysts would be complaining that what the team really needed was harder running backs and a quarterback in charge who knew what he was doing. Year after year we rated high offensively — in 1965, for instance, we were fourth in the league but first in offense, averaging thirty-one points per game — yet we would lose half our games because the opposition managed to outscore us. We led the league in points scored that year, 421 (in fact, only half-a-dozen teams in the history of the NFL have scored more points in a single season, and each of those was a title winner), but we also ran second in the opposite category, points scored against. It would be unfair to our defensive teams of those years to say that they had never played well. We did have spurts of very fine defensive play. But in order to maintain a winning team, the defense has to be consistent. It is actually more important than a consistent of-

155

fense. An offense isn't going to have a super ball game every week of the season; on the off days a good defense can still keep you in the running.

Nolan proved to be a man of his word. I hustled my tail off in training camp. During the exhibition games, Mira, Spurrier, and I all put in equal time. When the season opened, whatever Dick's evaluation methods were, I got the nod.

It turned out to be a very rewarding year for me. We had a fine new receiver, Clifton McNeil, acquired in a trade from Cleveland, who caught seventy-one balls that season to lead the NFL in 1968. For the team it was a transition year, a building year. We finished third. We played good offense. And I had proven to myself that I could still play top football. Nolan had agreed to judge only my ability to play the position, and I had done a good job.

When my throwing arm began to give me a little trouble again, toward the end of the season, I didn't regard it as a danger sign. I didn't regard it much at all. By the end of any season, everybody's hurting somewhere. You ignore most of it and keep on playing. Hell, I had thrown a football maybe fifty thousand times. That in itself is bound to affect your arm sooner or later.

During the off season I didn't notice my arm because I wasn't throwing a football. It didn't bother me seriously until training camp opened in 1969. From that point onward, the more I threw, the more my shoulder hurt. I couldn't figure out what was wrong. Every time I lifted my arm it ached so much it would go weak. It got to be like lifting a girder. I couldn't put anything on the ball. I was afraid my arm was gone for good.

The trainers tried to work with it. Linc Kimura rubbed my shoulder down every day. He tried whirlpool baths, he tried cold packs and hot packs and mud packs. Nothing eased the pain. Finally I tried some codeine, just so I could keep working out. But my game was definitely off. Lloyd Milburn, our team physician, told me it was tendinitis and recommended rest to avoid all irritation of the inflamed area. So I spent a couple of early season games sitting on the bench nursing my arm and watching Steve Spurrier call the plays.

Then I switched to another pain killer, and I could play again. I started taking a beautiful little green pill called Dexamyl. It not only eased the pain to a point where I could throw the ball as hard and as far as I wanted to, it keyed out everything but what was happening right there on the field. It put me totally inside the game. For the last seven games that year I felt I was playing as well as I ever played in my life. I started out taking half a Dexamyl before the game started. Soon I was taking one. Then it was one in front and another one at half time. By the end of the season I was taking one before practice too. The medication wasn't solving anything. It just controlled the pain temporarily and kept me in a state of suspension, where I really didn't have to deal with anything besides football.

In the off season I kept taking Dexamyl. Any time a problem came up I would pop one of those little green babies and feel a whole hell of a lot better. I told myself it was to ease the pain in my arm.

Since that pain in my arm was what seemed to be my most serious problem, I went looking for help. Now obviously if I had been in another line of work, this arm

157

ache would have been no cause for alarm. I could have learned to live with it. But when you're a quarterback, no arm means no job. I saw some doctors in the Palo Alto area. I tried cortisone for a while. I talked about some kind of operation. In March I flew to Los Angeles to see Dr. Robert Kerland, the team physician for the L.A. Rams, who was looked upon as the best in the business when it came to athletic ailments. He examined me and began by telling me the same thing others had said, that it was an inflammation due to severe tendinitis. He recommended rest and some light exercises that might gradually rehabil-itate my shoulder. In the process, he intimated some-thing I already half suspected — that this condition, al-though physical, might be something which would take more than exercise or rest or time to cure.

"I can't really tell you it's going to get better," he said. "There is no structural problem here that I can see, other than the inflammation. I know it hurts, and you might just have to live with it."

Without saying so directly, he implied that I myself had somehow created this problem, and I myself would have to solve it.

Back home I took some medication he had recom-mended, I followed his three-month program. It didn't do much good. Meanwhile I was talking to other doctors, hoping for some other diagnosis that would lead to a cure. I heard several, but nothing worked.

When training camp opened in July of 1970 I was on Dexamyl again to get through the practice sessions. The stuff was becoming less and less effective, and now it wasn't doing as much for my game. But I had to have it in order to play. My confidence was undermined. I had

158

built up a mental as well as a physical dependency. Without the Dexamyl my arm would ache each time I lifted it to throw, and the ache would sap away all my strength. The pill killed the pain, so I could get through a game. I played the first exhibition this way. We lost it.

During the week after that game I stopped in at the insurance office in Palo Alto where I had been working part-time between seasons. My habit was to stop and chat with my secretary, Mary Roberts. She was in her late twenties then, very efficient and very reserved in almost everything except her attitude toward a system called Scientology. Her enthusiasm for this was boundless. Whenever the opportunity arose she would encourage me to look into it. She wasn't a missionary, but she genuinely felt it could help my arm. I distrusted it completely. I was scornful and would challenge everything positive she had to say about it.

She had first recommended Scientology to me in 1968, when the early signs of this shoulder trouble began to appear. From the way I described the pain to her, she suspected that its origins might be more than physical. She had recently become involved with Scientology, and she had a specific person in mind she wanted to introduce me to. I laughed. I had just read two articles in *Life* magazine. The first, entitled "Scientology: A Growing Cult Reaches Dangerously Into the Mind," described it as a kind of psychological con game. The second, entitled "A True-Life Nightmare," was written by a New York playwright who enrolled for the program and ended up feeling cheated and burdened with more difficulties than he had gone in with. I had read the articles carefully because I was still groping around, interested in anything that claimed to enlighten people about themselves. This sounded to me like just another cure-all gimmick, a mental medicine show, made worse by its name. Any word that ended with *-ology* was not to be trusted — an attitude that went back to my Stanford days. Ologies had always confused me, either because the ologists didn't know what they were talking about or I couldn't figure out what they were talking about.

I had told Mary then that I did not have time for such nonsense. I had told her so on a few occasions since, with rather sarcastic delight. In fact I had taken it upon myself to talk her out of this foolishness. My frame of reference was the two articles in *Life* magazine. That was all I knew about the subject, but that was enough to give me an inflexible opinion.

Being a patient and generous woman, Mary smiled her way through all this. When the condition of my passing arm came up on that afternoon in August 1970, she mentioned once again that she would be happy to introduce me to this acquaintance of hers. As usual, I scoffed. I reminded her of the articles in *Life*.

"John," she said, "you don't believe what the newspapers write about the Forty-niners, do you?"

"Hardly ever."

"Then why do you put so much faith in something you read in a magazine, when you've had no experience with the thing itself?"

We had been through all this before, and she knew I didn't have a comeback for that one. I shifted to ridicule.

"What the hell will he do anyway, stick wires up my nose? I heard that the whole deal came out of a science fiction novel someplace."

"Phil has a method for helping you understand what's going on inside your own mind, that's all."

This was getting close to what put me off most about the whole idea. I scoffed at what sounded like gimmickry; mainly I scoffed because I was afraid of anything that could expose what was inside of me. I wanted to know. But I didn't want to know. I was challenging Mary now, going through my list of objections because secretly I wanted her to talk me into it. I had been aware for some time what a stronger and happier person she had become. It showed in her manner, in her openness toward other people. She was more able at her work, and she appeared to be a whole lot better off than I was. No job-crippling ailment to grumble about; she wasn't going around attacking things she didn't understand. Although I didn't tell her so that afternoon, I was beginning to see that she might be in touch with something I didn't have. Maybe she knew more about what was good for her than I knew what was good for me.

Before I left the office she said, "When you're through with the doctors and trainers, and if none of that seems to work, remember that I do have a friend who would like to talk to you about it. His name is Phil Spickler."

I played the second exhibition game on Dexamyl, and by that time I was fed up with the way things were going. My arm was getting worse. My dependency on the drug was increasing. I felt like a walking basket case. I kept thinking of Dr. Kerland's message: the problem was something I myself might have to solve. The next week I went back to the office and told Mary I might be willing to talk to this Spickler fellow, whoever he was. I saw it then as a last resort. I was desperate for something to

161

change. "I don't know if he can do me any good, and I don't really expect him to do me any good," I told her. It was almost a dare. "I'm not asking for miracles either. But if you think he's okay, maybe it's worth my time to talk."

Loosening Up

14   PHIL SPICKLER had been involved with Scientology for about seventeen years. Not long before I met him he had given up his career as a civil engineer and had been ordained a minister in the Church of Scientology. He was not the kind of minister I expected. When I called at his house, he greeted me with a smile that was in no way pious or evangelical. He wore sporty clothes — a cardigan sweater, flared slacks, open-necked shirt. We could have been two golfers meeting by chance at the first tee.

We talked casually for a while about the reason for my visit, my problem, and what his approach to it would be. Then we adjourned to a small, private room, and he asked me to sit down at a table. He sat opposite and brought out a hinged wooden box with two wires attached and two small metal cans clipped to the ends of the wires. Before we got down to my case, he explained the contents of the box. He called it an electrometer, a simple device — like a minipolygraph — powered by a small, rechargeable battery. It measured galvanic skin responses. I would hold

163

the cans in my hands, and he would ask me questions and watch a needle on the face of the box. My feelings would affect my skin responses, and by watching the deflections of the needle, Phil would be able to tell which subjects, which questions carried the greatest "charge" and thus needed more exploring.

This was one of the strangest moments of my life. I had had my bones x-rayed. I had had my chest listened to through a stethoscope. But never had I been connected to an electrical device that was supposed to be able to measure my emotions — my fears, my trouble spots, my confusions. I felt extremely vulnerable and exposed in a way I never had before. I had been wary to begin with, still skeptical. Now my skepticism mounted. I'm sure this in itself sent the E-meter's needle flying. I was ready to bolt out of there and go back to my bottle of little green pills. But another part of me was intrigued. I've come this far, I thought, I might as well go through with it.

Also, there was something about Phil himself that I felt I could trust. He was thirty-nine at the time, a gentle and soft-spoken man, the kind of guy who gives everything plenty of time and a kind of guy I had not come across much in my travels as an athlete. He wasn't trying to prove anything, or win anything, or make anybody's team.

He assumed that my arm wasn't this sore for this long merely from throwing a ball. He started out by asking me if it had ever given me any trouble before, if there were any earlier events involving my arm that came to mind. It didn't take me long to remember half a dozen. As a child I had slammed into a fence gate that was supposed to be open, and I had broken the collarbone on my right side. Then there was the auto accident in 1963, when I broke the forearm, and the second break during that Minnesota game a few months later. And of course there was the constant pummeling quarterbacks take from opposing linemen who go out of their way to rough up your throwing arm. This had been a condition of my life. I told him about one play in a game against the Colts when Big Daddy Lipscomb, God rest his soul, left me on my hands and knees with my arm half wrenched from its socket and a tooth knocked out.

That was all we talked about during our first meeting. But by the time the hour was over, my arm felt better than it had in months. This was enough to bring me back for a second session. It seems so simple, looking back, but I had never examined these moments in my life or made any connection between those previous events and my present ailment. It was amazing to me. In my arm something had actually started to loosen up. Inside me, something else had started to loosen. I didn't know what it was until I had met a few more times with Phil.

By watching my responses on the E-meter he quickly saw that the auto accident in 1963 was carrying a heavier charge than anything else we were discussing. He zeroed in on that. At our second meeting he asked me to begin at the beginning, to describe it in as great detail as possible. I did so, recounting the late drive home from the bar, swerving on the curve, smashing into the tree, coming to in the hospital and trying to convince the people in emergency that it wasn't just my face that needed attention.

When I finished the story, Phil was still getting a high charge on the meter. He asked me to go through it again, looking for more detail, to dredge up as much as I could about the incident. I told the story again, and then a third time, and then something popped into my conscious mind that had never been there before.

"On the way to the hospital," I said, "someone sitting next to me looked at my face, and then at my arm, and said, 'Well, that poor sonofabitch will never throw a football again.'"

"Who was speaking?" Phil asked.

"It must have been one of the attendants," I said. "Nobody else was in the ambulance."

"But I thought you said you were unconscious until you got to the hospital?"

"I was," I said, astonished. "I *was* unconscious. How the hell could I hear something like that if I was out like a light?"

"Well, you heard it all right," Phil said. "It's just been locked in there for a long time."

This was what Phil had been looking for, what they call in Scientology an "engram," a traumatic and formative moment that has somehow been repressed yet continues to affect your behavior in ways beyond your control. The ambulance attendant's prediction had been simmering in my unconscious for seven years, agitating all my deepest fears of declining ability or failure. It had finally surfaced as this psychosomatic ailment in my throwing arm. Phil made me tell the story again and again and again, until no charge showed on the E-meter.

That weekend we played the Denver Broncos up in Portland in another exhibition match. Just to be safe I took a Dexamyl before the game. I threw for three touchdowns and realized afterward that, as far as my arm was concerned, I could have played without the drug. My arm was feeling better all the time. But my confidence

166

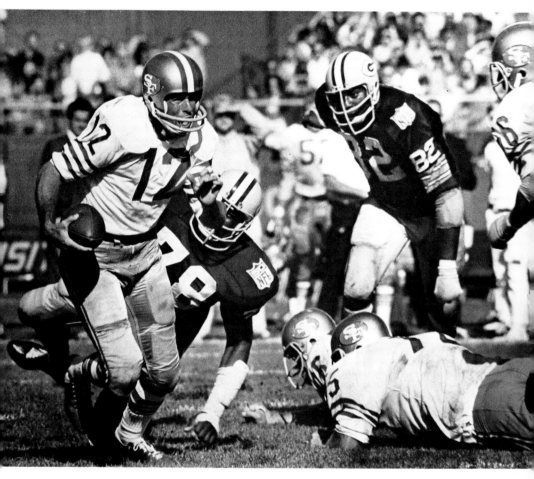

I never did care much for running with the ball. There was always
somebody like Lionel Aldrich, No. 82, Green Bay's defensive end,
trying to discourage me.

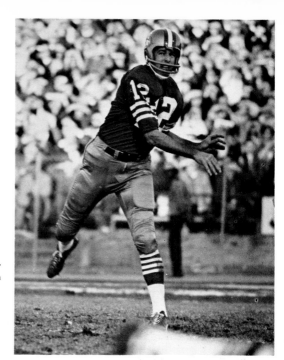

This is what I call good protection.

Photo by and courtesy of Ray De Aragon

"If a quarterback's mind is on the rush, there is no way he can execute the play." I tried to explain that to Coy Bacon of the L. A. Rams, but he wouldn't listen.

I also tried to explain that to Darris McCord, No. 78, and Roger Brown when we played Detroit in 1965, but they wouldn't listen either.

Photo by James Drake, for *Sports Illustrated.* © Time, Inc.

Talking it over with Woody Peoples.

Photo by Fred Kaplan, for *Sports Illustrated.* © Time, Inc.

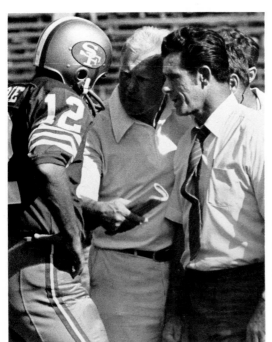

With Dick Nolan (right) and Ernie Zwahlen, offensive line coach.

Photo by and courtesy of Ray De Aragon

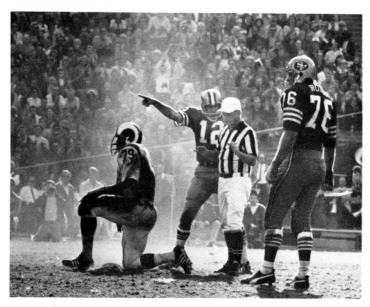

I never had an argument with an umpire in my life. Photo by and courtesy of Bill Nichols

I was just about to make my move. Dave Robinson, Green Bay's linebacker, made his first.

Photo by Heinz Kluetmeier, for *Sports Illustrated.* ©Time, Inc.

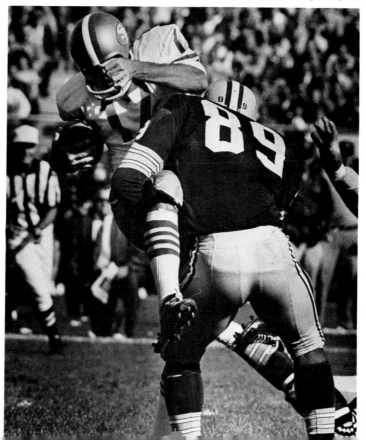

One more run with Merlin. Seems like this is always the way it was between us.

Over the years Deacon Jones and I got to be very close.

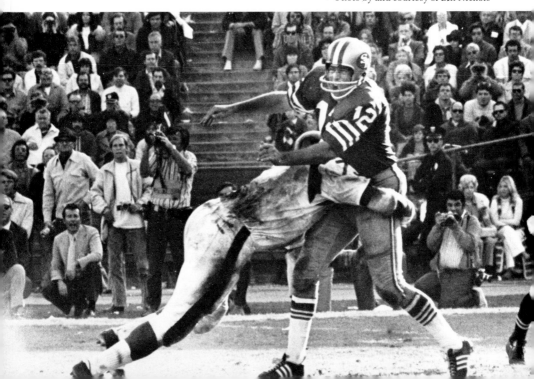

Our final game at San Francisco's Kezar Stadium, December 1970, when we lost the conference championship to Dallas and missed the Super Bowl by seven points. The next season we moved across town to Candlestick Park.
Photo by and courtesy of Bill Nichols

One of the great moments of my life — scoring the winning touchdown against Detroit in 1971, when we won another division title.
Photo by and courtesy of Bill Nichols

A swing not beautiful, but mine.
Photo by and courtesy of Bill Nichols

With Lanny Wadkins and John Miller (center) at the Crosby Tournament, Pebble Beach, California, 1973.
Photo by and courtesy of Jimmy Dale

The Brodie brood, spring 1974. (Left to right) Kelly, Erin, Diane, Sue, Cammie, and Billy.
Photo by Jonathan Huie

was still shaky. Mentally I was still dependent on the stuff.

At my next session with Phil, we came back to the auto accident. He didn't ask me to go through the whole thing again. Instead he asked me to imagine the accident itself occurring in a slightly different way. "Imagine," he said, "that you are coming down that road, losing control on the curve, heading for the tree — and then, instead of hitting the tree, you drive right through it and keep on going."

I tried it. I closed my eyes and saw myself approaching that massive oak. I didn't lunge for the floorboard this time. I didn't grope with my foot for the brake pedal. I drove my car into the tree, through the tree, out the other side, and sat there steering while my car took off like an airplane. It left the ground, with me behind the wheel, and seconds later I was flying my car in slow, easy circles above the tree. And I was laughing. There in the office Phil was laughing with me. We were both laughing at how good it felt to be on the other side of that tree and free of it at last.

Each of these sessions lasted an hour. At the next one, he had some other images for me to explore.

"Imagine," he said, "that your arm is a weapon. It *is* a weapon, after all. You are out there every weekend trying to use it to deceive some cornerback, to defeat the other team. Think of it as every kind of weapon you can imagine."

I ran through it in my mind. Working my arm back and forth there in Phil's office, I imagined it as a rifle, as a flame thrower, as a bow and arrow, as a howitzer, as a grenade launcher, a spear, a broadsword.

Phil was not just making up games for me to play. His

167

idea was that you can sometimes relieve an affliction by exploring how you yourself have afflicted life or have affected others. It was a matter of opening up my imagination a little. One step in rejuvenating my arm was to open my mind to what the arm had been through.

"Here's another way to think of it," he said. "Every time you throw that ball, you are letting go of something. Something is being released. Perhaps in a way it is being lost. Try to throw those passes in reverse. Imagine that you are recovering all those passes, pulling them back into yourself."

I tried it. I was sitting at the table, pulling my hand back toward my ear, replaying old football games, symbolically recovering energies I had lost or had feared I was losing.

Finally Phil began to talk about the communication lines between my brain — my central computer — and my other body parts. "Sometimes they get snarled," he said. "An event like that auto crash can disrupt the normal flow of output and feedback. Certain parts of the body can actually start to atrophy," he said.

He asked me to imagine the internal linkages, from fingertips to brain, from brain to fingertips, to legs, to toes, etc. He asked me to close my eyes and turn various parts of my body into different substances and then to visualize my whole body and to tell him if any parts of it looked dark, or darker than the rest. I had some dark areas, and he told me to change them to gold. My right arm was the darkest part of all. When he told me to imagine it as golden, I concentrated on this. Soon I saw the veins and nerves and bones in my arm coursing with a kind of golden light. It was a hot, electric, golden flood. My arm and shoulder felt hot as lava.

168

I opened my eyes. The image dissolved. I began to
swing my arm loosely back and forth and around my head.
It felt light, totally unburdened. A great weight had been
lifted. It felt back to normal.

"That's incredible," I said.

"No it isn't," Phil said. "You wanted your arm to get
better, and you found a way."

"How long is this going to last?"

"There's no reason to think it's a temporary thing. Just
go use it."

"You mean I can start throwing?"

"Isn't that what you want to do?"

Let's Have a Go at It

15 THAT WEEKEND we played the
L.A. Rams in our final exhibition game. For the first time
in almost a year I went in without amphetamines. My
arm felt better than normal. It felt better than it had in
five years. I was twenty-one years old again and throwing
the football all over the park.

From that point on, two things were happening at once.
I continued to meet with Phil twice a week, figuring that
if his auditing could do that much for my arm, it would be
worth finding out what it could do for the rest of me. And
football became more enjoyable than ever before.

I don't believe in miracles. I do believe in an individual's ability to know more. This is what it boils down to:
the more one knows about himself and his work and the
people he deals with, the more he can achieve. What
happened in Phil's office wasn't a miracle cure. It was,
rather, my first moment of true self-knowledge. I'd had
no idea how much one shoulder could weigh, how much
freight it could carry. All the tensions in my life seemed
to have centered in one little area of about eighteen

170

square inches. Taking the pressure off that arm led into a process of understanding that is still going on, because getting well meant getting *more* than well. I found out that my arm problem was related to a very limited notion I had about myself and about life. Curing the arm, in fact, was just a fringe benefit, the first stage in opening my mind to wider possibilities. I had to change the way I perceived the world, the way I thought and felt, and the ways I treated others. Life was a larger and more interesting affair than I had ever imagined.

Eventually this process would take me right past football. But in the beginning, in 1970, I still had some games I wanted to play. Everything I was learning I tried to apply on the field. Just knowing, for instance, that with more awareness I could close that gap between what I did on the field and what I did off the field, and that there was a method for achieving it — knowing this in itself was a kind of liberation. Along with my revived arm, it gave me new energy. My enthusiasm picked up so much that I found myself in agreement with just about everyone. I no longer had to defend my own point of view; I could look for ways to find the best point of view for everyone involved to get the job done. I began to see the game through a wider lens. Unhampered by many of my most obvious fears and hang-ups, I could *be there* all the time, with all my attention focused on the game. In the past this had been an ability that would come and go. I couldn't rely on it. Now my perceptions just seemed keener, my mind uncluttered.

It happened that this personal rejuvenation coincided with a few other developments inside the 49er organization, things that had been getting ready to happen for the past two years. Dick Nolan turned out to be an exceptional defensive technician; I had watched him draw more Xs and Os than anyone else in football. He had brought all his expertise to the task of building up a powerful defensive team. And Ed Hughes, the offensive backfield coach, had worked hard on our passing attack. His whole life was detail, the specifics. Every week he would come up with a list of fifty pass plays he had devised with an eye for the opposing teams' defense and personnel. He would check these with Ernie Zwahlen, the offensive line coach, and with Jim Shofner, the receiver coach, and cut it down to a list of maybe thirty, which he would then show to me. I would select the ones I liked best, maybe seven or eight that seemed to me to give us the strongest advantage in the game coming up. Then at the end of the week, Shofner and I would go over all these. I would explain to him why they appealed to me, perhaps offer some suggestions of my own, and he would feed this information back to all the people concerned with offensive play. Thanks to Shof, who became my voice to the rest of the coaching staff, communication lines were better than they'd ever been before. Going into a game, we all knew what we were going to do, and why. Because the team got off to such a fast start that season, the staff continued to allow me to go out and do things pretty much my own way.

The team itself was young. We had a lot of guys who had been there for two or three years, and this happened to be the year when it all came together. Two outstanding receivers had joined us in 1969 — Ted Kwalick, the All-American from Penn State, and Gene Washington, from Stanford, who was now my roommate on road trips.

172

Among the older veterans who had survived the changes of the late sixties was Ken Willard, still playing fullback. In five years he had established himself as one of the NFL's most consistent power backs. Ken was also an aggressive blocker and a fine receiver, thus the ideal fullback for the kind of football we were playing. When we weren't throwing the ball, he was the guy we'd hand it off to. His best plays were the blunt and the draw. There was almost no way we couldn't make five yards any time we needed it, just give the ball to Ken.

We were a passing team. The whole offensive line was geared for this. The gaps between our linemen were the smallest in the league. They gave me plenty of time to set up for those long bombs to Kwalick and to Gene. In fact, they set a pass protection record that year. I only got caught with the ball eight times all season.

We had a bunch of players who were ready to go. We had a solid defense and a simple, workable offense. By the time we completed the exhibition games we were tuned up and charging into what became the best season the 49ers ever had — the first of three title-winning seasons in a row. I had been waiting a long time for this, and it was sweet. I loved every minute.

The first game we played the Washington Redskins and beat them, 26-17. I never felt better playing football. Bam, bam, bam. Everything was going right. The next week we played the Cleveland Browns, and somehow I had the feeling we were going to win. It didn't matter; I mean, I wasn't obsessed with winning, and the whole mood of the team was loose, that kind of freedom from the compulsion to win that makes it so much more possible to play to the utmost of one's ability and thus have a greater

chance of winning. We beat them, 35-33. I can recall
that with three minutes left to play, I threw a pass to
Jimmy Thomas for about sixty-one yards and a touchdown, and that was probably as good a ball as I have ever
thrown in my life.

The offensive team adopted a sort of slogan that season:
"Let's have a go at it!" To me it signified the spirit of the
group. It was not a grit-your-teeth and do-or-die attitude.
"Let's have a go at it" meant we were ready to do the
best we possibly could and at the same time have a little
fun at something we all enjoyed doing.

When we lost the third game to Atlanta, 21-20, nobody
was devastated by it. We made some mistakes, and we
kept on going. The next week we played Los Angeles
and beat them, 20-6. We had not beaten L.A. since 1967.
Now we had a 3-1 season, tied with L.A. for first in our
division, and things really opened up. We had been predicted for last place when the season started. After the
L.A. game we went all the way to 7 and 1. We were in
first place and ahead by a couple of games. We flew to
Detroit and got our butts kicked 28 to 7. But nobody was
uptight. Then we played L.A. again, and this time they
beat us good. That loss hurt, really took the wind out of
our sails. A lot of people started saying, "Well, there go
the Forty-niners. This team isn't any different from all
those other ones. This is what always happens. They got
all the way to seven and one and then blew it. They
always find a way to get their ass whipped in the end."

One big difference was the presence of the new players
on the team, who were not too familiar with this 49er
"tradition." Guys like Cedrick Hardman, Forrest Blue,
Cas Banaszek, and Kwalick and Washington — they didn't

174

have time to listen to all those predictions of doom. Also, Roosevelt Taylor had been traded in from Chicago, where he had played safety on a lot of championship teams. He was not about to assume that we would be losing it in the clutch. Taylor, together with some of the veterans who had made it through the 49ers' lean years, provided a lot of stability and positive thinking.

We came out of this slump the following weekend, in our second game against Atlanta. I can pinpoint the moment when we turned it around. It was midway through the third quarter. They had just kicked off to us after scoring their third touchdown. We were behind 20-7. Bruce Taylor took the kick-off and had a little trouble getting started because the turf was slippery. Someone had decided to try a reverse, and what happened, Bruce and Preston Riley ran right into each other. The ball went flying up in the air, and Atlanta recovered on our four-yard line.

Talk about deflation. While Nolan jumped up yelling, "Who the hell called that goddamn play?" we sat there on the bench certain that Atlanta would now take it in for another score. In our minds we had already given them that fourth touchdown and we were wondering how we were going to win it from twenty points behind — when one of our defensive guys broke through and hit their halfback Harmon Wages such a lick that *he* fumbled. Suddenly we had the ball back. An electric shock ran through the bench. The feeling was, "Jesus Christ, if we are *ever* going to play football, we got to get with it right now, because this is the biggest break of the century!"

It brought us back to life. We took over on our own five and ran it right down the field for a score — 20-14. Then

175

we got the ball back on our own fifteen and ran it down again, eighty-five yards, to take the lead, 21-20. About a minute and a half remained in the game, and some of the guys started getting uptight, saying, "Okay, let's not do anything foolish. We got the game. Let's don't lose it."

Well, hell, I had been on the losing side of about eight teams where the controlling thought had been, when the going gets tough, pull in your horns and make sure you don't make any mistakes. If I had learned anything from those experiences, it was that the thing to do at a time like this is *make things happen.* Because we didn't have the game yet. A field goal could beat us.

We were back on our own thirty. I told Washington, "Gene, just run on by that safety." And he did. It was fake blunt to Willard, then I dropped back and threw Gene about a fifty-five-yard pass that he took to their twenty-yard line, and that was where the game ended.

The next week we beat New Orleans. Then we drove across San Fancisco Bay to Oakland and beat the Raiders 37-7 on their home field, which gave us the division title — a gratifying game for all of us, but especially gratifying for me, since Oakland was like my second hometown; it's where I had started playing football.

Things were moving so fast that season, there was such a flow and forward motion, it almost seems now as if we flew directly from Oakland back to Minnesota for the divisional play-off against the Vikings.

I have never been around a team more keyed up and ready to have a go at it then the 49ers arriving in Minneapolis in the dead of winter. The thermometer showed eight degrees. We never noticed the temperature. We trotted out onto the field in our short-sleeve jerseys, which led the press to report later that we were "psyching out" the Vikings with this show of disdain for their climate. Actually we only had one set of game jerseys ready, so those were the ones we wore.

Snow was piled up behind the end zones, glinting in the sun. We could have cared less. Bud Grant's Vikes had the best season record in the league. They were predicted to go to the Super Bowl. Nobody had expected the 49ers to get nearly this far, and nobody gave us a chance that day, except us. We were a little like those teams Frank Albert threw together in the late fifties, used to winning games no one expected us to win. We were so wired up we would have played the Yukon Polar Bears on an ice floe if it meant getting one game closer to the Bowl.

It turned into a back-and-forth ball game, without a lot of scoring. They scored first, picking up a fumble and running it in for a touchdown. We scored once and then kicked a field goal. After that our defense was so tight they couldn't get a first down. Neither team could get into another scoring position until the last few minutes of the game. What happened then I suppose can be blamed in part on the weather up there in Viking territory. They say extremes of climate can do strange things to people. I know I have seen some pretty strange things happen in Minnesota in December.

In 1965 we played the Vikings on the ice, and we beat them, 45-10, mainly because we wore tennis shoes, while Norm Van Brocklin made his guys wear cleats. It was the damnedest thing I'd ever seen — linebackers sliding around like they were on roller skates; those poor guys couldn't do *any*thing. And then, during this 1970 play-off game, some of the Vikings came sneaking over to use our

177

heaters. Our benches were on the same side of the field. Bud Grant wouldn't let his team have any heaters out there. So one minute I'd be up against some guy who was trying to tear my leg off; the next thing I know he is scrunching up right next to me trying to keep warm.

The game was almost over when Bruce Taylor, our cornerback, ran a punt return to their fifteen. Ken Willard picked up about six yards, then Doug Cunningham took it to the four for a first down. Two more line plunges by Willard brought the ball to their one and a half, and we had a third down and goal to go with less than two minutes to play. We also had a 10-7 lead. A score at this point could sew up the game. Settling for a field goal would not be satisfactory. It had to be a touchdown. And because of the momentum behind this series of plays — four solid short gainers — we felt certain we were going to make it.

My head was working. I jumped back into the huddle to get the next play in motion as fast as I could. And, Christ, there were only four of our guys grouped up. Forrest Blue, the center, was over talking to the ref. Our two ends, Ted Kwalick and Dick Witcher, were about to square off because Kwalick was explaining to him how similar this was to something that happened when he was playing at Penn State. "This is just the way we did it at Penn State, man!" And Witcher was glaring at him, saying "If you don't shut up, I'm going to take your Penn State and stick it right up your ass!"

Over to my left I saw Ken Willard standing next to Doug "Goober" Cunningham, our running back, and Willard was ready to take him apart, because Goober, who is from Mississippi, was giving out some kind of rebel yell,

178

"Yee! Yee, yee!" in the direction of Wally Hilgenberg, the Vikings weakside linebacker. "Hey, Wally, you want some more a that? Huh? Huh?"

Willard yelled at Goober, "Would you shut up, you little hillbilly sumbitch, and get on over here!"

And Goober yelled back, "Hell, we got 'em, Ken! We got 'em!"

There we were, going into the most important play in the history of the franchise, and the whole team had fallen to pieces with excitement.

If I didn't call a play in a couple of seconds I'd have to call a time out or get penalized. I didn't want to call time when we were moving the ball right down their throats. I looked at Woody Peoples standing next to me, the only cool head on the field at that moment.

"We can't call time," Woody said. "You just run it over me."

Woody was our right guard and all business. He seldom opened his mouth in a huddle and never said anything he didn't mean. He was playing opposite Gary Larsen, who some people said was the strongest man in football. But if Woody said he could open a hole there, I knew he could do it. I had no other choice. It was the only play we could call with only two men listening.

I yelled out, "Okay, everybody line up!"

Forrest was already standing over the ball. The rest of the guys crouched down at the line. Forrest snapped it. Woody drove Larsen back about three yards, and I tumbled into the end zone for a score. The Vikings came back a minute later and scored too. But it wasn't enough. That play had given us the winning touchdown. The play-off game was ours.

179

It was the first time I had run a quarterback sneak in five years. Afterward the reporters wanted to know how I dreamed up that play from a yard and a half out, since this is a pretty long shot for a sneak. I told them we had noticed a visible crack between our guard and center and had just been waiting for the right chance to exploit it.

BEING THERE

IN THE HEAT and excitement of a game, a player's perceptions and coordination will sometimes improve dramatically. At times I would experience a kind of clarity which I have never seen adequately described in a football story. Time itself would seem to slow way down, in an extraordinary way, as if everyone were moving in slow motion. This happened to me in a game against Chicago. It seemed as if I had all the time in the world to watch the receivers run their patterns, and yet I knew the defensive line was coming at me just as fast as ever. The whole thing seemed like a movie or a dance in slow motion. It was beautiful to watch.

Sometimes you discover that defensive players are in a similar state, and then the game actually moves up a level. In that Chicago Bears game, Dick Butkus and I had a real thing going. I was in a very high state, and by the end of the game I was grinning every time I came out of the huddle. Finally he looked across at me — he was only about three feet away once we got lined up — and he said, "Wipe that smile off your face, you chickenshit sonofabitch."

181

He was calling defensive signals. I was at a level where I just *knew* what their defense was going to do. Butkus knew what it was like. When he said that, he was tipping his hat to me. I have paid him similar compliments.

There are times when an entire team will leap up a few notches. Then you feel that tremendous rush of energy across the field. There is nothing mystical about this. When you have eleven men who know each other very well and have every ounce of their attention — and intention — focused on a common goal, and all their energy flowing in the same direction, this creates a very special concentration of power. Everyone feels it. The people in the stands always feel and respond to it, whether they have a name for it or not.

This isn't unique to football. Attuned people in almost any endeavor talk about similar highs. But I'll tell you what happens to football players. They achieve this state of what I call *beingness* much more often than is generally recognized — while they are on the field. But all too often, after the game is over, or after the season is over, they lose it. They don't apply this involvement in other areas of life off the field. So after a game, you see them coming down, making fools of themselves sometimes, coming way down in their tone level, going all the way down, after they have been all the way up.

Making Things Happen

16 WHAT MADE THAT SEASON and the next two so enjoyable for me was that "Let's-have-a-go-at-it" feeling on the team together with what I myself was able to do out on the field. A quarterback is a kind of juggler. The trick is to keep a whole lot of Indian clubs up in the air — or floating in your mind — and the more experience you have, the more Indian clubs you can juggle. My first play as a pro, in 1957, I couldn't think about much else besides making sure I had a good grip on the ball. Pretty soon you get all those incidental details under control — breaking the huddle, getting the numbers barked out right — and you've got the playbook in your head, hoping you can call the right one at the right time. But you can't really do that effectively until you *own* the plays, until you know why you call each one, when it's best, and whether or not it still looks best when you get to the line of scrimmage, and if not, where to go from there. And this means learning to juggle all the other details you have continually to take into account: the score, the quarter, the down, yards to go, time remain-

183

ing, the number of time outs, the weather, the wind, the conditions of the field, the condition of your men — who's high, who's low, who's hurt — and also the condition of the men on the other team — who's strong, who's not so strong, who's slowing down.

To bring it all together, to make one play appear out of all this, the quarterback ideally needs to be *inside* the game and *outside* the game at the same time. He has to be up close there at the line of scrimmage, looking into the eyes of the middle linebacker, who is three feet away and squinting out through the bars in his face mask trying to figure the next move, and he has to have enough detachment to consider patterns on the field moving in time, like a living chess game.

I had been able to do this before 1970, but with irregular control. Sometimes I was so much *in* the game, I couldn't look *at* it. In 1965 I had learned a whole lot and I had been part of an operation that was working at top efficiency, and I knew how it had to work. But I had not really been in control of it. That was the difference between 1965 and 1970. I guess that's a way of explaining the difference between making All-Pro in 1965 and being selected for the Jim Thorpe Award and the Most Valuable Player in the NFL in 1970. My lens had widened so that I could make things happen on the field and rely on my ability to do so. This was what made those games in the early seventies so rewarding.

Here is the kind of thing that would happen. A team might have ten real good plays you never call because the right situation doesn't come up on the field. Or a defense might have a tendency that you'll save a play for until the moment when that tendency can be turned into a weakness. I considered it the ultimate satisfaction, playing quarterback, when I could spot such a situation and fit the play to it, or better yet, create a situation that could exploit a certain play or a hole in the defense.

We did this a few times, for example, during the Oakland Raiders game in 1970, when we clinched the division title, because they had a defensive setup that was ready-made for our passing attack. They played a man-to-man defense, and they played it in such a way that we could always occupy their free safety. Studying the films before that game, I saw that in a short yardage situation, say, third down and a yard or two to go, he would be responsible for helping the linebacker on a hole in the middle of the line and also for keeping up his man-to-man responsibility in the secondary. Depending on how the play went, he could be drawn in toward that hole.

We reached a point in that game where we had the ball on about their thirty-five, and it was second down and four to go. I was pretty sure Ken Willard could do what he always did and make those four yards, plus a couple more, and get us a first down. I also knew we had a pass play that was a sure touchdown if we could get to a third down and one inside their thirty-five. I always felt that the best place to score from on a pass play was somewhere between the other team's forty and twenty. Once you're inside the twenty, it's harder to get a ball to your receivers, because there just isn't much room; you've got too many people in a shrinking space. It's a one-on-one game there, and you have lost most of your wide receiver opportunities. Throwing from back the other way, say from behind your own forty, the receiver might catch a pretty long ball and still get tackled around the ten-yard

185

line, and you have to go in from there. Whereas the same
play from inside their forty will take you all the way. So
there we were, on Oakland's thiry-five, and I'm thinking,
"Why go for a first down when we can set it up for a
score?"

In the huddle I told Ken, "Don't go for a first unless
you know you can really take off. Try and stop about a
yard short."

He knew what I was talking about because we had
gone over all these options during the week before the
game. He slammed through a little hole that opened up
and got himself stopped about one foot short. You don't
usually rejoice when your man fails to make a first down.
I was so pleased I almost laughed out loud. It was right
where I wanted it to be. On the next play I called a fake
blunt, which drew the free safety forward to cover Willard, who seemed to be plunging into the line to make
that one foot we needed for a first. Gene went long, and
he was so far in the clear it was comical. Oakland had
some fine defensive backs that year, but not one of them
could cover Gene by himself. He was just too fast and
tricky. It was more responsibility than any back could
handle. With the free safety suckered out of position, it
was like picking daisies. I tossed him the ball, and he
galloped in for six.

Gene Washington played an important part in all that
was happening to me and to the team during these years.
John David Crow had been my roommate from 1965 to
1968. Then he left the team. Gene was drafted the following season and was my roommate from 1969 on. Although he was twelve years younger and, in many ways,

186

as different from me as anyone could be, we had a lot in common. He had gone to Stanford and had played quarterback there for two years before they switched him to end. We saw eye to eye a whole bunch when it came to football. His experience as a quarterback gave him a valuable perspective as a receiver. He knew how the field looked from where I was standing, and that helped him explain to me how the field looked to him and what worked best for him.

Just as John David and I had spent long hours talking about the intricacies of backfield play, so Gene and I would spend whole afternoons and evenings — generally in a pleasant surrounding — going over pass patterns. We both agreed that this kind of intense conversation was more than beer-drinking shoptalk; it was an important part of being as prepared as possible for what happened during the game. It became a kind of rehearsal of the dozens of possibilities and combinations we might be up against on a given day. Where is the best place for Gene to go in such and such a situation? Where is the best place to throw the ball? How would his pattern change if this defense appeared?

We would draw a picture of two defenders in a given zone and talk about ways he could beat them. You don't need a lot of patterns to do that. You just need one good solid idea that the passer and the receiver can agree on. The difference between a good receiver and a great receiver is his ability to find open spots when they are trying hard to cover him, when the defense is paying close attention to that one receiver's every move, doubling up on him the way they had to do with Gene. He finds those openings by taking apart the patterns the way we would do. We would break it all down into three or four basic possibilities that we both understood.

I would ask him, "Gene, can you read this kind of defensive setup? Can you tell the difference between when they are here and when they are here? Is it clear to you every time? And can we make this little shift without ever getting our signals crossed?"

We would trade questions like that until we were so thoroughly prepared and on the same wavelength all this became second nature to us. We got to know each other so well we could actually communicate decisions on the field simply through eye contact. You might say that we turned the *audible* into a *visual*.

Coming up to the line, Gene would scan the defense and think, "In this situation, I could run such and such a pattern." To the degree that we had already foreseen this setup and worked it out, I would know where he was going. I learned to believe in our ability to read the same defense in exactly the same way. If you tried to do this with an entire team of eleven men, you might well go insane and end up getting demolished. There are just too many ways the signals could get confused. But between two men we could make it work a high percentage of the time.

We connected on some fantastic passes, and for a while it led to some speculation in the press that we had transcended the ordinary means of communicating from one ballplayer to another and that mystical forces were at work on the field. There was one play in particular, at Candlestick Park, when we were playing the Redskins in a divisional play-off. It was a long pass to Gene in the end zone, so long that it seemed — Gene said later — to

188

hang up in the air for about twenty minutes. Then it seemed destined to fall right into the hands of Pat Fischer, the Redskins cornerback, who was a step in front of Gene. Fischer in fact was in a perfect position to intercept. But an instant before it touched his fingertips, the ball took a little jump, and arced over his outstretched hands and into the arms of Gene for a score.

Amazing.

But not mysterious.

Just a good mixture of preparation and luck. All you really need to know to explain it is that the wind was howling through Candlestick at about forty miles per hour. And it was raining. The field was wet and slippery as hell. It was one of those days when anything can happen. They were beating us 10-3, when we got into a third down with one yard to go on our own twenty-one. In the huddle I called for a fullback blunt. But I told Willard to be ready to go either way, to take or fake it. I told Gene, "Hey, if it looks good, I'm going to call an audible. So be ready for it."

What I meant by *good* was a pattern that would put Fischer playing Gene by himself — something that would develop if the free safety moved far enough forward to cover the possible line play. Fischer was a super little defensive back, but they had put a lot of responsibility on him. With third and one, this deep in our own territory, we were going to have everybody coming up pretty close. From where I was looking, it was another one of those times when you tend to pull in your horns so you won't make any mistakes — which is precisely what can defeat you. If we didn't create something very soon, make something happen out there, we were going to careful

189

ourselves right out of the play-offs and right into a 10-3 loss.

When we got up to the line of scrimmage I saw that it was not exactly what I had hoped for. The secondary wasn't pulled up quite as far as I had expected them to be. I didn't audible. I started my snap count. And as I did, the defense began to shift. The free safety started moving forward the way I had hoped he would. Now I didn't have time to audible. It was one of those moments when I looked over at Gene, who had also observed the shift, and we both knew what he was going to do, which route he was going to take to get past Fischer.

When there are two people going downfield and one of them is Gene, you know you have an awful good chance of getting the ball to him. It was a little tough to throw. Everything was getting slick. It was one of those throws you just feel your way into, right through a cross-field wind. That's why it hung in the air so long, and that's what lifted it right over Fischer's fingertips. He's a good back, he was in just the right spot to intercept, and probably *should* have intercepted, but the wind was on our side that day. Gene caught it running and took it in, which turned the game around, and we won the play-off, 24-20.

They Have to Give
You Something

17 DURING OUR WINNING YEARS the peak game for me was the last regular-season match in 1971, against Detroit. I would go so far as to say it was the single most satisfying game of my whole career.

All through that season, people kept counting us out, just as they had the year before. And we just kept counting ourselves in. We knew we had a winning ball club. Near the end of the season, L.A. lost a game everyone thought they were going to win, and that put us half a game in the lead in our division. If we won our last two games, we could win another title. We beat New Orleans, and then we had to beat Detroit. It was a historic match, in a way, because the 49ers had been in a very similar situation in 1957, playing Detroit for a title. That time they had beat us, 31-27. Fourteen years later the score was the same, but this time in favor of the 49ers. We played at Candlestick, and it was a ball-buster of a game.

Two of their defensive coaches, Jimmy David and Dick Voris, had spent some time on the San Francisco staff, so

191

they had a lot of dope on us. We also had a lot of dope on them. Detroit's defense, which they had helped shape, was much like one the 49ers used to play. The week before the game, I spent a lot of time talking to some of our defensive guys who remembered how it worked — Ed Beard, Charlie Krueger, and Mel Phillips. They had played that defense and had ideas about ways to beat it. They explained, for instance, that a certain kind of run between the tackle and the outside linebacker put a heavy burden on both tackles and the other linebackers. It was not a weakness in the personnel but a feature of the system. I filed that play and put it in my pocket with a note about just when we might be able to use it.

Meanwhile we were giving a lot of thought to the ability of their offense, which was impressive. They had Greg Landry at quarterback, a hell of a player when he's throwing well, which he was. They had Charlie Sanders at tight end; and Mel Farr, running back from several Pro Bowls; and Steve Owens, young Heisman Trophy winner who had come on strong at fullback; and Earl McCullouch, who was so fast some of our linemen swore he could run the hundred in 4.6 seconds. They were going to score some points, there was no doubt about that. We figured we were going to have to go out and throw a lot of footballs and pile up more points on the board than they did.

We were primed for this one. Then, while we were warming up, one of those little things happened that you can't plan on at all, but if you are prepared everywhere else you can cash in on it right away. Al Clark, a Detroit cornerback, came up to Gene Washington and said, kind of proud of himself, "Gene, it's just you and me today, baby. You and me."

They Have to Give You Something

There is so much banter being thrown around before a game, you get into the habit of ignoring it. But Clark said this like he meant it. Gene looked at him, trying to see if he was serious. Then he looked at me.

As Al loped away I said to Gene, "Just you and me? He has to be kidding, doesn't he?"

Gene grinned and shrugged and hoped it was true. And I grinned, thinking, "Sonofabitch, if he's playing Gene man on man, we're going to have a go at it right *now*, for the whole rest of the day!"

A good defense can sometimes camouflage exactly what they're doing, and how they're doing it, and why. So on our first series of plays, I threw a short, outside pass to Gene just to test this rumor. Sure enough, Al Clark was on him, and Gene made about eleven yards. He came back to the huddle saying, "Yeah, that's the way I like it. Make sure you don't change anything all day long. Just you and me, baby, you and me."

A while later I tried it again, a short out, and we connected again. So I said to Gene, "Hey, let's save this one. If we overdo it, they'll take him out of the game. Let's save it for when we need it."

Clark was a rookie, a fine cornerback, but young. There was no way he could cover Gene on a short pass to the outside. So I just put that card in my pocket and held on to it.

I had a whole handful of cards that day. You might call that one my hole card. If it hadn't been that one, I would have found another one, because every defense has to give you something. Certain backs, for instance, will just watch the receiver. Others will just watch the quarterback, and feel the receiver. Others will watch the quarterback for one second or for three steps of the movement

193

and then they'll pick up the receiver and watch him the rest of the way. The more you know about how a man plays, the better you can take advantage of it. A team that plays man to man and is always looking at the receivers should be extremely vulnerable to end runs; and the receiver just leads his own defenders right out of the play. Atlanta had four real aggressive linemen who would blow across the line and sell themselves out trying to get to the quarterback, reading any running play that developed on the move. They were quick and powerful. Well, you can fight that, or you can look for plays that turn all that force to your own advantage — draw plays, quick traps, draw traps, certain kinds of tackle traps that let them go whichever way their energy takes them.

Beating a defense, when you get right down to it, means beating people. This is one of the simple principles of the game. When disagreements would arise between me and the coaching staff about ways to move an offensive team, it would usually come down to some fundamental issue like this. I have never felt that the game was that complicated. You figure out what your team can do best, rather than what is fashionable this season, or what is trickiest, or what looks good on paper, or appeals to the sportswriters. Then you find out what the other team has got, what their individuals can do. You have to give some thought to their *system*, of course, but beating a defense means beating specific people who are trying to work inside that system. You apply your strengths to their weaknesses.

After the Detroit game got under way, every once in a while I would throw one of those short outs to Gene. It wasn't a big yard gainer, but it was a sure thing. My theory was, don't get greedy; take what they give you. When you take what they give you for long enough, this creates a frustration. They will try to plug that hole. This in turn creates another opening somewhere else. I started looking for how they were going to cover this. I knew they'd have to do something. They weren't going to change their whole pattern, they were just going to compensate a little. They urged Al to play Gene a little tighter, and pretty soon Wayne Walker, the outside linebacker, was edging over a step or two to sort of give Al a hand.

What you want to do is get somebody concerned with having to cover what you know and he knows is weak. Then he has to make some compensation which you can take advantage of in another way. Now Wayne Walker and I had been playing against each other for fourteen years. He knew me inside out, and I also knew a little bit about him. He is as tough and as smart as they come. He is not going to make any mistakes. But the very fact that he *is* so dependable makes him predictable. I knew what he had to do in that situation, and that made him vulnerable. When part of him is trying to cover those short passes that the wingback can't quite handle, this gives us just enough opening in the line to set up some solid runs by the fullback to the weak side. Then we have them coming and going. We've got them between a rock and a hard place, and no matter what they do, they are going to have to give us something somewhere else.

Like we figured, it turned into a high-scoring game. We built up a fast lead, 17-6 at the end of the first quarter. In the second quarter they got ahead of us 20-17 because Landry was playing our defense like we were playing

195

theirs. After their third score we got the ball back on our own thirty-five, and in about five plays we ran it on down to their thirty, playing that combination, a couple of quick outs to Gene, a couple of fullback blunts. Wayne was trying to cover for Al Clark. Then he'd have to worry about covering the blunt. So Mike Lucci, the middle linebacker, started trying to help Wayne out. On one play in that series we ran a fake on the same blunt play and I threw a delayed pass to Kwalick down the middle, just to keep the linebackers honest. By the time we got to their thirty-five we were in a perfect setup for the final play in this drive.

It was third down and about six to go. After this whole series of short gainers, it made a lot of sense, from one point of view, to go for the first down and make sure we kept control of the ball, since if Detroit ever got it back they were sure as hell going to do what they had already done three times and run it down for another score. But I was also thinking that a touchdown pass to Gene was almost a certainty from this situation. Wayne was playing it a little bit loose, because he didn't figure we could make six yards running. He wanted to be ready to cover the short out. Al Clark had been caught just enough times that he would be on the double alert for that. When you have a guy who has been beat short two or three times, he has to do something to make up for what he has allowed to happen. For his own self-respect he has to figure out a way to stop it. When you have beat a guy short a couple of times you can almost go to the bank on his determination to make a big play out of what he's been getting beat on. So instead of going for the first, which is what Wayne is expecting, in one form or another, and instead of going

196

for the short out, which Al is ready for, I called an out-and-up — the pattern where a wide receiver fakes a short out, heading toward the sidelines, then cuts farther downfield. It was a way to take all that determination Al Clark had waiting for us and turn it to our own advantage.

It also happened that we were pressed up against the sideline, which, contrary to what some people think, is the best time to throw an out-and-up. The wingback knows he has you pinched, so he doesn't stand right in the way of the receiver, he stands a little inside. He's using the sideline, thinking he's in a good position to bump the receiver toward the sideline just when he turns. If he has a lot of space to cover, he won't give you that much. It allows a good receiver just enough space to get around him when it's time to make his move.

I called the play and dropped back. Gene cut out toward the sideline, and Clark had his eyes glued to Gene to see what he was going to do. I didn't look over that way until I was ready to throw. When I turned, I cocked my arm, just a fraction of a second late, and went completely through the motion of throwing, really pumped my arm, so that Clark took his eyes off Gene and looked at me in order to follow the ball. Clark's impulse to cover the short out gave Gene a step downfield, and when I let the ball go, a moment later, he was in the clear. He took it twenty-five yards for another score.

It is pure delight when you can bring off something like that, to foresee it, then make it happen. The timing is crucial, the way you take the ball, get your steps, start to throw, do everything to throw and yet the ball's not gone. Gene knew just when I was going to look, when he had to make his move, all those things we had talked about in

197

such detail, those little moves, which sometimes don't
look like anything but which make all the difference between winning and not winning, between beating the
good teams or not beating the good teams.

After that series we were ahead 24-20. Detroit scored
again, making it 27-24 — an offensive ball game all day
long. It was late in the fourth quarter when we had one
last shot at the goal line. At that point, it was a slightly
different kind of play; that is, it was a matter of controlling
the ball as tightly as possible. Detroit had run the ball
from their own twenty down to midfield, where they had
a fourth down and half a yard to go. The percentages say
fourth and one is not a good time to run for it in that situation. But there was also a strong feeling out there on the
field, and the feeling was, goddamn it, we'd better control
this football, because if we give it to them, they are going
to score. They tried for the first, and they didn't make it.

When we took the field and took over the ball, it was
with the strongest surge of confidence and strength on a
football team I have ever felt, like all our adrenalin was
just pumping out from a common source. We knew we
were going in, and we started moving on the ground.
First Ken Willard would take it through the middle; then
Larry Schreiber, our rookie running back from Tennessee
Tech, would take it through. The line was making holes,
and Ken and Schreiber took turns finding the holes, eat-
ing up the yards, two and three and four at a time. We
did this for fourteen plays, while five minutes of game
time ran out on the clock. Finally we got it to their eight-
yard line, with about forty seconds left to play.

It was third down and goal to go, and I dropped back to
throw a pass to Ted Kwalick in the end zone. They had

198

him so bottled up I could barely see his jersey. I looked for Willard, to hit him on a swing pass, but he was jammed up too. No other receivers were open. Suddenly there was nothing else to do but run with the damn thing. I had ten yards to cover and had to get past Walker and Mike Lucci. They were both converging on me with good angles to make the tackle. One of them surely would have nailed me, but hallelujah this once for Astro-turf and the puddles it leaves lying around on that un-beveled field at Candlestick Park long after the sun comes out — both of those men slipped. Wayne went to lunge for me and lost his footing and fell on his hands. By the time he got his traction I was in for the winning score. I was almost laughing out loud at the sight of those two guys falling down like that and knowing we had won the game — because we hadn't left the Lions enough time to get back at us. It was one of the great moments of my life.

Afterward some people thought that it was a called play — just like the quarterback sneak against Minnesota. It wasn't. We won that game, and our second title, by coming up once again with the right mixture of those tried and true ingredients: all-out teamwork, total preparation, split-second timing, and shithouse luck.

STATISTICS

BOOKS LIKE THIS often carry some kind of career summary listing all the awards and statistics of the player. I'm going to leave that part out. In the case of the quarterback, statistics can be too misleading. I have been at the top of the NFL passers' list, I have been in the middle, and I have been near the bottom of the list. I have broken records, and have had my own records broken, and I have found that very little of that record-keeping corresponded to what was most important in the progress of a game or a season. The statistics can measure how many passes you have thrown and how far they went. They cannot measure the difficulty of a situation on the field and how a quarterback handled it.

Physical ability to get the ball into the air is necessary; it's a given. You have to be pretty good at that to get into this position in the first place. But the top quarterback is not the guy who can hit a bull's eye from forty yards away, he is the guy who can do that and also coordinate everyone else's abilities to move the ball and get it into the end zone. There comes the time when all hell is breaking

200

loose, the coach is kicking the bench, the players are yelling and swearing at the ref, the fans are standing up yelling and screaming, and somebody has to put some mortar into it and make something happen. And he isn't necessarily the guy who can throw the tightest spiral. A guy can look mighty pretty throwing passes. He can complete more passes than anyone in history and still not be getting the job done. One of the ironies of record-keeping is that almost every guy who has really thrown for thousands and thousands of yards has spent a lot of time with a losing team. Why? Because you are behind, and your only chance of catching up is to throw the hell out of the ball, take risks, hoping for the long score.

Too much concern for statistics can get you playing for the wrong reasons. Statistics themselves can actually get in the way of the game. In 1970 we were playing the New Orleans Saints at Kezar Stadium. The game was tied 20-20, and we needed it real bad. It was the fourth quarter, we were in the middle of downfield drive, and I had just completed a twelve-yard pass to Doug Cunningham, which put us on the Saints thirty-yard line, when the officials stopped the game.

I thought, "Jesus, who was *that* penalty on?"

One of the refs came over and handed me the ball. I asked him what he was doing. Then an announcement came over the PA system telling the crowd that this last pass had put me over the 25,000-yard mark. Only three other quarterbacks had ever accomplished this, they announced — Y. A. Tittle, Sonny Jurgensen, and John Unitas. I was being awarded the game ball.

Well, I honestly did not know I had crossed that line. I had never kept track of such things while I was playing.

201

And it was not a show of false modesty when I seemed confused by the announcement. What was most on my mind was the ball. They wanted to award me the ball and then take it out of the game.

I needed that ball. I liked it. I could throw it comfortably. If they brought in another one, the game would be over before I could get it broken in. A new ball has a tacky kind of resin or lacquer they cover the outside with, supposedly to help you grab it. Actually this makes it slippery as hell, and until you get the ball rubbed down and broken in, it's liable to fly around some. The best way to get a ball into playable condition is to rub it in the dirt. That particular ball had three quarters' worth of dirt and grass and sweat worked into it so that it really felt good in my hand. And here they had stopped the game in the middle of our drive, and now they were going to take my ball away.

I felt like saying to the ref, "Hey, as long as it's my ball now, why don't we just keep it out here on the field for a while."

But I couldn't. Forty thousand people were cheering that line I had crossed. I had to toss the ball over the sideline and hope we could pick things up where we had left off. We didn't. The game ended 20-20. I would have gladly cashed in a few thousand of those accumulated yards for one more point that afternoon.

Eight Ways to Survive

18 As I said, from the beginning of the 1970 season two things were happening at once. On the field, football was better than ever. Off the field, I was meeting with Phil Spickler twice a week in those hourlong auditing sessions. For the first six months, nobody but Phil and Mary Roberts, the secretary who introduced us, knew I was doing this. I was too self-conscious about it to tell anyone else. I was actually embarrassed for any of my colleagues to know I was dabbling with such a thing. And I was still a little cautious. I'm a very inquisitive person. I don't mind deciding to try something and I don't mind giving myself up to it — because I know from experience that's the only way you find out whether or not it works. But I like to reserve the right to get out if I don't like the way it's going. I didn't want to announce that I was "into Scientology" and then have to turn around and announce that it was screwed and I was getting out of it.

I didn't even tell my wife. Two nights a week I would just disappear for three or four hours, without explanation.

203

I'm sure Sue suspected I was doing a whole lot more than going down to the corner saloon for a bottle of beer. She did notice that my arm wasn't giving me so much trouble. But she didn't know why. What finally tipped her off that something unusual was going on was not my unexplained absence but some noticeable change in my manner, in my attitude toward her and toward the kids. I was more accessible to them. When I was home I did not seem so preoccupied with things outside the home. I was more relaxed, more considerate. I was *there* and not somewhere else. She wanted to know if I was feeling all right. I told her I was feeling fine and then explained to her what I had been experimenting with for the past six months and that it was making me feel better and better all the time.

Before long she too was going in for auditing sessions with Phil. I didn't have to talk her into it. She had noticed a change in me, which she saw as a sign of growth, and she decided to try it for herself. She'd had tension headaches almost every day for years, and those soon disappeared. But like the curing of my arm, that was just a fringe benefit, a starting place. Within another six months, it led to a total re-evaluation of our relationship and what we were all about as people and as husband and wife. It has to be some kind of tribute that, after going through this, we are still together. I have seen more than one family break up after the quest for self-knowledge and greater awareness begins. The people involved suddenly discover they have absolutely nothing in common and never did, and they split. I watched this happen after that first seminar we attended down in Monterey; three or four divorces came out of that one. Which is not to say that the seminar was bad, or that a marriage is something to be preserved at all costs. I'm just thankful that ours survived. After four kids and thirteen years, Sue and I had, in some ways, grown pretty far apart, but it wasn't too late to get it back together again.

If I were to describe my world view before 1970, it would go something like this: you are born, you live, you die.

I took it for granted that I was here for a while, and that I was going to take a hike, and I would worry about that part of it when the time came, and probably not even then since it would be too late to worry. I had never seriously given much thought to what man is really composed of. I knew everything there was to know about football and little at all about the rest of it. In my personal life I had assumed that everything was "all right." Not good. Not bad. But as much as could be expected. If someone asked me, "How's Sue?" I would say, "Fine." "And how are the kids?" "The kids? Just great. Great." Well, the kids weren't always doing so hot. And Sue wasn't always fine. Every two years or so there would be a huge crisis; we would reach some kind of truce and suppress the problem and keep on going: I would retreat to the football field, and she would retreat into the care and feeding of the kids. I wasn't doing much for the betterment of my family. I had put a lot of money in the bank account, but I hadn't really given much of myself. I was avoiding most of my responsibilities there and building up resentments inside that were always about ready to explode. Somewhere I had lost the interest and enthusiasm for having a family. Somewhere I had lost the interest and enthusiasm for even having real friends. I sort of assumed that everyone I knew was "a friend" but that one never really liked another person. It was hard to like anyone else, because I didn't really like myself. Off the ball field, very little happened in any of my relationships that I could honestly call enjoyable. I was enduring people rather than enjoying them. I was enduring my marriage with a sort of stubborn tenacity.

All this gradually began to change as the result of my auditing sessions with Phil — or, as Phil would say, as the result of my decision to do something about the way my life was going: "I am not the doctor," he would say, "you are the doctor. You are the source of your own ailment, and you are the healer."

He and I would talk about other areas of my life, my past, my anxieties, etc., much like he had first explored the problem of my arm. We would go back along my time track looking for other incidents that might be having a negative effect on my present-time behavior, creating bad reactions, or mis-emotions. This is what it's all about, reaching an understanding of yourself so that you can function right now, in present time, to *be* wherever you are, whether it's on a football field, or alone with your wife, or talking to some kid who is trying to kick his drug habit (which is part of a program I have been spending a lot of time with since I retired as an active player).

Obviously it is not enough just to take apart what has happened in the past. You need some way of looking at or evaluating who you are and what you are doing now and as you live from day to day. After a while Phil began talking about what Scientologists call the Eight Dynamics of Life. Now, there are many ways to describe the various levels a man is capable of operating on. The Eight Dynamics came as a revelation to me because I had never given much thought to more than two or three of them. It opened me up to the range of my possibilities as a human being, and any system that can do that for you has to have something to offer.

It became a handy way for me to pinpoint the areas of my life that needed changing or improving. The two dynamics I had been most absorbed with for my entire life were the first, which is The Self, and the third, which is Groups: me and my football team. The second dynamic, which is your family and your sex life, I had sort of stumbled through like a man half asleep. The fourth dynamic, which is mankind or society at large, had never concerned me much one way or another. The fifth, which is other life forms, plants and animals — well, it may seem strange that a man can reach the age of thirty-four and never see a tree or a meadow as much more than an ornament or a tool to serve whatever man thinks he needs that for, but this was my condition. Grass was not a thing in itself, with a life of its own; grass was something you played games on, and it was better than playing on asphalt or polished wood because it didn't hurt so much when you fell on it.

The next three dynamics are the physical universe, the spiritual universe, and the Supreme Being, which is not something separate from man but something a person can become part of through his own spiritual growth.

The guiding principle behind all of this is to enhance survival, the survival of oneself, of a family, of groups, of mankind, and all other forms of life. The more I understand about myself in relation to each of these dynamics the better able I am to survive and to be a productive person.

When I finally reached the point where I could truly

grasp the meaning of this, it appealed to me tremendously. One of the main reasons I found Scientology so rewarding is that it helped me to voice ideas about the world that I had vaguely felt were true but never had the words for. It helped me bring into focus certain tendencies in myself that had been there a long time but were never entirely clear to me. The emphasis on survival, for instance. For twenty-one years I had been dodging monster linemen and beating out other quarterbacks, fencing with coaches and owners, and ducking beer cans thrown by hostile fans. My instinct for survival was finely tuned, yet I had only applied it in this one, somewhat limited, region of the world.

Then there is the belief in the innate powers of an individual to control his own life. You have to believe in something like that pretty deeply to imagine that you can ever be a quarterback in the first place. I had always wanted to be a *cause* rather than an *effect,* which is one of the basic distinctions Scientology makes in the way people relate to the world.

You might even say that figuring out how to handle the eight dynamics is another kind of juggling act but harder and more complex than juggling all that data on the ball field because you can't stop at the end of two hours.

It was a two-way deal. Meeting Phil Spickler when I did, this helped make me a better ballplayer. At the same time, the years I put in playing football gave me a kind of grounding in personal experience that allowed me to make good use of what Scientology has to offer. It soon became clear to me that I wanted to enhance my own survival. I wanted to grow as a person, on as many dynamics as I could, not merely on the football field. When you put all your effort into one or two of the dynamics, and neglect the others, eventually you undermine your own survival. My priorities, in short, were starting to shift. But this process had not yet reduced my interest in the game. For that matter, when I finally did quit playing, it was not because football had become less important to me but because other areas of my life had become *more* important.

As of 1972, though, that had not yet quite happened. After all, we still had a great football team, with two division titles in two years. We had come within eleven points of the Super Bowl, and almost everyone would be coming back — Ken Willard, Gene Washington, Ted Kwalick, Woody Peoples, Forrest Blue. You don't just walk away from an opportunity like that.

A Sea of Hands

19 NINETEEN SEVENTY-TWO was my sixteenth year in pro football. I was thirty-seven that August, which isn't very old in some parts of the world, but it is ancient for a ballplayer. Every time I stepped out onto the field I was breaking another longevity record of some kind — oldest man ever to throw three eleven-yard passes in the second quarter, most games played by a quarterback born west of Denver, highest single-game completion percentage by a man with a daughter in high school.

As the season started, sportswriters were comparing me to a bottle of vintage wine. "He improves with age," they would say. I like to think they were right. I still felt that I was improving. I also like to think I could have continued playing the game until I was fifty. That may sound ridiculous at first but only because no one has done it yet. George Blanda might. The qualities most important to good quarterbacking *do* improve with age. A receiver, by comparison, seldom plays more than ten years, because the qualities essential to that position are speed and

210

quickness in catching the ball, qualities that leave you early, especially after getting knocked around for a few years. A track man can go out and run and run and run and not lose his speed, but when you're getting your legs bapped around the way a receiver does, this starts to effect your speed and your spurts. A good running back is lucky if he lasts six.

A quarterback is different. Almost all the longevity records in the NFL have been set by quarterbacks: George Blanda, John Unitas, Y. A. Tittle, Earl Morrall, Len Dawson. Even after your arm starts to lose some of its zip, you can be worth a great deal to a team because your most valuable asset is your knowledge of the game, the ability to read a defense, to handle problems on the field — qualities that improve with experience. The deciding factor, really, is how long you can continue to take a lick, how long your body can stand to get hit. I admit I started to feel it during those last two years. The ground started to get mighty uncomfortable. I would get up groaning from blows I never would have noticed a few years earlier. Artificial turf had something to with that though. Plastic grass just doesn't treat you the same way. Sometimes I wondered if they had put any padding under there at all.

Apart from the arm I broke in 1963 — which happened *off* the field — I have never been injured much or missed many games because of injury. I broke a big toe at Stanford in 1955, but that happened during spring practice and just gave me some free golfing time when the weather was good. A shoulder separation, lower back pains, miscellaneous cuts and bruises, a couple of broken teeth — nothing to write home about. In 1972 I was in-

211

jured twice, causing me to sit out half the games. Maybe it was a warning that my time had come. Certainly this was a contributing factor to the change in my status on the team. It gave Steve Spurrier a chance to play a whole lot. He had been waiting in the wings a long time, and he had some good days. In nine games he threw eighteen touchdown passes.

I got injured first in the game against Buffalo. I sprained my right wrist in the second quarter and was out for the rest of the day. It was okay by the following weekend, when we beat the New Orleans Saints, 37-2. Two weeks later we were playing the Giants in San Francisco and losing badly. Right at the end of the fourth quarter, in the last thirty seconds of the game, I had dropped back to pass to Vic Washington, our running back, waiting for him to get into the clear, and waiting for the patterns to form, and waiting, and just as I was ready to cut loose, Jack Gregory, the Giants' tackle, broke through and nailed me. My left foot was planted, and a little too far forward, and it didn't move when Jack plowed into me. My body moved, my leg moved; my goddamn foot liked it there in the grass, I guess. I could feel the tearing in my ankle as I fell and a hot rush of pain as I lay waiting for Gregory to get up. They said later it was a sprain. I knew it was worse than that. X rays showed that the lateral ligaments were stretched all over the place. For the first and only time in my life, I was carried off the field in a stretcher. For the second time during a regular season I was bound up with a plaster cast.

For the next three weeks I was on crutches. When they took the cast off, I was another three weeks getting my leg back in shape. I spent those games up in the spotters' box, along with Doug Scovil, the offensive backfield coach, and we relayed play information down to Jim Shofner, the receiver coach. I admit it was hard sitting up there with my foot in a sling watching Steve win ball game after ball game. I was rooting for the team, of course. We had worked out a good system for sending down a lot of the plays that helped Steve move the ball. But he was the man on the field, he was hitting Washington and Kwalick for yardage, while I was up there watching the chessboard from high above, sidelined with leg trouble, feeling my age. And they don't make it easy for you — the sportswriters, and the fans — when you're injured in the middle of your sixteenth year. IS BRODIE THROUGH FOR GOOD? would be the typical headline. It's hard to ignore. It plants a little seed. It also toughens your resolve. I was a long way from finished, I told myself.

I suited up for the game against the Rams but didn't play. The following weekend I suited up again for the game against Minnesota and almost didn't get to play in that one. I was really feeling good, completely recovered, and dying to get in there. It was the last game of the season, and as usual with the 49ers it was a cliffhanger situation. We had a 7-5-1 season record but still had a shot at the division title. Everything depended on this Vikings game. If we won it, we'd have our third title in a row.

Near the end of the third quarter we were behind 10-6. I had watched it all from the bench, waiting for Nolan to give me the nod and getting more and more agitated because I felt I should be on the field. When the Vikings scored the third time, Dick told me to start warming up.

By the time I got into the game we were in bad trouble, behind 17-6 with a quarter to play. Disappointed fans, feeling failure in the air, were already leaving the stadium, more interested in beating the traffic out to the freeway than in sitting dismally in the rain to watch this game wind down to its inevitable end. It brings me back to that theory about the high-yardage statistics. In a situation like this, there is no time for caution. There was only one way to go, and that was to throw the football like it was a hot potato I couldn't wait to get out of my hands. In ten minutes I threw fifteen passes.

There was another motive to my seeming recklessness. I got into the huddle, and the team was as tight as a turtle shell, sort of pulled up inside itself and afraid of making a mistake. They were so tied up they couldn't speak, so worried about winning there was no way, in such a condition, that we could have won anything. We had to loosen up or we were finished. My attitude was much like it had been in 1955 the day I went into that game against UCLA when we were so far behind there seemed to be no way out. So what if we lost the sonofabitch! We might as well have a go at it on our way down. I was like the man caught in the water a mile from shore; if I don't think I can swim a mile, I'm not just going to gurgle to the bottom, I'm sure going to find out how far I can swim before I drown.

The first pass I threw was intercepted. When we got the ball back, I did it again, threw a second interception. More grumbling fans were on their way up the aisles. When we got the ball back the next time we were on our own one-yard line. That was when things started to click. I kept throwing the ball on every play. The team caught

214

fire at last. We moved it ninety-nine yards for a score. It was as crazy and wide open a quarter as I've ever played. With four minutes remaining, the Vikings had to punt from their own twelve, and one of our guys got penalized for defensive holding, which gave them the ball again. They ran it down to our forty-eight, then they got penalized for holding and finally punted out, and we got the ball back on our own thirty-four, with a minute and a half to play, and the score now 17-13.

I kept on throwing, and we took it down to their twenty, where I threw one to Vic Washington, who caught it on the seventeen and ran it all the way to their two, fighting for every yard. I had completed nine out of twelve, and they knew I was going to keep on tossing it. They had us boxed in so tight, the first two went incomplete. On third down I called a pass to Dick Witcher, our tight end. The Vikings were playing soft and were kind of expecting the pattern, but Witch made a great adjustment on it. He and Charlie West, a Viking defensive back, were heading for the corner, and West was beating him there, so Witch just stopped and turned around, with Charlie behind him, and caught the ball in the end zone.

There were only thirty seconds to go. We had won it, 20-17, and Candlestick Park was out of control. When the gun went off, fans came tumbling down out of the stands, pouring across the field. Before I could get away, a gang of them swarmed around me, for a moment dragging me along as they grabbed for my arms and legs. One of them damn near choked me to death before they got me hoisted up onto their shoulders, carrying me toward the players' exit. I felt like I was dangling up there, some huge rag doll being jiggled and joggled along. And I was concerned. Half of them were drunk, all of them were insane with victory, roaring and howling with delight. Hands were reaching toward me, grabbing at me. I didn't know what the hell they were going to do with me. I just held on tight.

It is a great tribute, of course, to be carried off the field by frenzied fans, one of football's honors that had never come my way before that rainy afternoon. It is actually rather amazing, looking back, to realize how much things had changed between me and the fans, in their attitudes toward me, and vice versa, from the early days of the shotgun when I was booed almost every time I blinked. The booing, which had gone on intermittently for ten years, was nowadays drowned out most of the time by cheers. But I had been immersed in noises from the stands for so long I seldom heard any of it anymore. In the intervening years I guess I had gone through just about every emotion a player can have toward those noises. At first it had hurt me deeply because I didn't understand it. Later on I grew to hate the booers. Then I got to the point where I learned to feed on it, as a way of stoking myself up for a game. I could channel their antagonisms into my own on-field anger — which made it easy to get charged up for any home game. At times I had used the booing as an excuse for having a bad day: "How can I play in a town like this?" I would silently ask. "How could anyone play where he is so disliked?" By the seventies I had grown past all that. I was even booed a few times during the best season the team ever had, and I just laughed. I knew by then where it was coming from. I had reached a point where I genuinely liked all the fans; I was appreciative that they came out to watch us

216

play, whatever their motives. I think, in the long run, this was another benefit of playing in the same city for all of my seventeen years. It was something like a marriage. Instead of leaving when it got rough, looking for a smoother situation, I had to learn how to cope with it. In the process I learned a lot about myself, my own limits and tolerances.

I went through all those changes of feeling, and by the end of my career we had come to understand one another pretty well. I could take their boos and I could take their cheers and not get too depressed or swellheaded either way. During the Minnesota game Spurrier had thrown three interceptions. They had been booing him without mercy. I knew what he was going through. He was the goat out there for that afternoon. They took it all out on him. When I started warming up along the sidelines, a great ovation had come rolling across Candlestick. I was the hero, the old pro throwing away his crutches to pull this game out of the fire. I admit it felt pretty good. Spontaneous ovations on my behalf had been few and far between in my own hometown.

Now they had me up on their hands and shoulders, yelling my name, the shouting, tumultuous fans, five or six hundred of them. We had come a long way together, the fans and I. The team had come a long way too, with a third division title to shout about. It would have been a good time to quit. Right there. Being floated out of the stadium on that sea of hands.

WINNING

VINCE LOMBARDI used to say, "Winning isn't everything, it's the only thing." Grantland Rice often quoted a famous line about its not mattering whether you win or lose, but how you play the game. My own view of the subject is somewhere in between these two.

You play to win. There's no doubt about that. But if winning is your first and only aim, you stand a good chance of losing. You have the greatest chance of winning when your first commitment is to a total and enthusiastic involvement in the game itself. Enthusiasm is what matters most. If I was enthusiastic about the game, enjoying it, and doing my absolute best, then I had the best chance of winning it. But then I could also handle losing, because I *had* done my best. If you can't handle losing, you'll never be a big winner. It's never easy to lose. But if I knew I had performed at the top of my ability, with total involvement, that would take care of the winning or the losing.

I haven't always felt that way about it. I know what it's

218

like to be obsessed with winning, to be obsessed with proving to someone else that I could play this game at such and such a level and could compete at such and such a level. At some points earlier in my career, winning or losing was so important that playing the game became a by-product; and of course this made it next to impossible for me to win anything.

The desire to be number one can be very dangerous. If being number one is your first motive, you always end up stepping on someone else to get there. Which means you can't ever really enjoy the accomplishments of someone else playing the same position. You can't enjoy his performance because you are always watching to see if he's better than you are. The goal, it seems to me, is to be as good as you can be. If this makes you number one, fine. If not, you haven't lost anything, and you have gained a lot. You can enjoy what others do. You can respect the qualities that are involved in doing the job. You can really wish the other guy well. It's awfully lonely being number one if you have had to fight your way upward through a pecking order with that goal in mind. Out on the golf links, where I have spent a good deal of my time, I have found that the best players are also guys who actually root for the other guy's shot. This kind of player enjoys the game, he enjoys all the qualities involved in the participation of it. He is not rooting against his own shot; he still wants to win. But the more positive energy you bring to the field of play, the better your own chances are.

Golf provides another interesting comparison here. Football is structured so that one team rises to the top of the heap. You have twenty-six teams in the NFL. One is the winner. The other twenty-five are losers. So you have twenty-five bunches of guys who feel inadequate and second-rate and frustrated, and their lives have no meaning because they didn't win the Super Bowl. And you have one bunch of gloating, self-satisfied hotshots strutting around grinning like idiots. It's crazy. Whereas, in a golf tournament, say you have twenty-six guys entered. Here is the guy who comes in fifth. They don't call him a loser. They say, man, you're doing all right, you're doing fine. They also know that the first spot moves around from month to month, and everyone understands this. There are too many variables you have to cope with on a golf course for the same guy to win all the time. So you have a lot of guys who are regarded as winners, and a lot of other guys who may not be winning top money but still they are not regarded as losers. Which is why I think the outlook for golf is pretty healthy. It is relatively free of this compulsion to "win" at all costs. Anyone who is making a good living out there is a winner. In fact, the same thing is true of football, or ought to be. The players are all men who have devoted a lot of their time and energy in the pursuit of something important to them, and they could all feel fulfilled if they could see the game this way. All pro football players are winners. In my opinion.

Moving On

20 THE 1972 MINNESOTA GAME would have been a good time to quit, because almost everything that happened to me afterward — as far as football was concerned — was kind of an anticlimax, a winding down. From that time on, it was never very pleasant. It wasn't unpleasant either. It was something else. It was . . . awkward. For the first time in my career I was feeling a little bit out of place. It had partly to do with the coaching staff, partly to do with the way the team was going, partly to do with the way my own mind was going. The decision to retire was a little like the way a play comes to mind: twenty factors influence the decision, and you make it and you move on it.

The turning point was the play-off game against Dallas the weekend after we beat Minnesota. Dallas was becoming our nemesis. It's funny, for a guy who chose to spend his whole life in California, how much of my fate has been settled in Texas. John David Crow went to Texas A & M. Y. A. Tittle comes from Texas. Bud Adams comes from Texas. Tom Landry and those goddamn

221

Dallas Cowboys came from Texas, and they just kept coming and coming.

We had played them in 1970 for the National Conference title, and they beat us, 17-10. They went on to the Super Bowl, and we came dragging home. We met them again in 1971 in the same situation, playing for the conference title, and they whipped us again, 14-3. In 1972 we played Dallas during the regular season, on Thanksgiving Day, and we really stomped them good, 31-10, on their home field. We met them in the play-offs, high from that Minnesota victory, sure we were going to clean house on the Cowboys once and for all.

And we *had* them beat! Going into the fourth quarter it was 28-10. Then Roger Staubach came off the bench to take over at quarterback for the Cowboys and he started doing exactly what I would have done, I guess. He was throwing the ball every way but down. That's when we blew it. We got so knotted up about not making any mistakes, we got so concerned about preserving our lead, that we lost it. I just could not believe it was happening to us the way it did. With two minutes to go in the game we still had them, 28-17. But in those last two minutes, they scored twice and came from behind to beat us, 30-28. A heartbreaker. A real deflater.

I can remember Charlie Krueger saying in the locker room, "Well, we just gotta pick up the pieces." We had been saying things like that to each other for years. I said, "Yeah, that's what we gotta do." But this time I didn't mean it. It was like, we can pick them up, all right, but putting them back together is going to be mighty hard work, maybe more work than it's worth.

I see now that the third straight postseason loss to

Dallas was when my enthusiasm started to turn away from football. It wasn't that I loved the game any less, it was just that I could no longer bring to it the total energy and effort it would take to overcome what I felt had allowed this defeat to happen. Playing football had been my "whole life." I could not honestly describe it that way any longer. My interests were changing and expanding, and there were other areas of my life to put some of this deep effort into.

At home I was trying to spend more time with my family. Between seasons I spent several weeks at the Scientology Center in Los Angeles, going farther with my auditing and beginning to think seriously, for the first time, about the future of this country and what steps a person might take to help it survive. What appeals to me most about Scientology is that it does not oppose anything. It does not define itself by being *against* something else. The whole thrust is pro-survival.

One thing had become very clear to me: you have to start within. The better you know yourself, the higher your level of awareness, the more effectively you can function as a person and as a citizen. Having begun this process for myself, I wanted to help others if I could. If I ever went into coaching, for instance, I would bring this kind of thinking to the task — my knowledge of the game itself plus my awareness of the frustrations and anxieties players are prone to, which can inhibit their playing and which often derive from insufficient knowledge about themselves and what they are doing in the game.

In March of 1973 I became director of the Narconon drug abuse prevention center in Palo Alto on the assumption that if we don't solve the drug problem in this country, we aren't going to be able to solve much of anything else. The idea in Narconon is to work on helping an individual improve his communication level and other basic life skills so that he is less prone to drug dependency and more effective as a person. If, for example, he is taking drugs in order to *be somebody,* we help him find a self-image that will allow him to achieve this without the need for drugs. I know this much: it works. This has always been my yardstick, on the field or off the field — whether or not something is workable. Narconon has worked in prisons, where it originated and where about half its centers are located. It has worked in communities from New Jersey to Hawaii. And it has worked in schools, where we are now setting up prevention programs through our Palo Alto center.

At first I did not really see these involvements as a part of the process leading to my retirement from football, even though sportswriters and others were suggesting that perhaps the time was "right." I knew damn well I wasn't going to be pressured into retiring by such hints and rumors. If I *did* retire, it would be when I made up my own mind to. I had thought about it more than once, of course. You have to, when you reach a certain age. People won't let you ignore it. People talk about the "right time" to quit, as if you should stay awake nights computing just the ideal moment, astrologically, to make this move, which depends on a concept of rightness that has nothing at all to do with how a player relates to the game, only with how the public relates to his reputation and the memories fans can carry around with them later on.

224

I have always admired John Unitas's opinion on this subject. "Why should I quit?" he used to say. "I have played this game because I enjoyed it. People tell me to quit while I'm ahead, while I'm still a hero. I didn't start playing the game because they viewed me as a hero, so why in hell should that be a reason to quit?"

The "right" time, as I said, and as some commentators suggested in the papers, would have been at the end of 1972. I didn't see it that way. I still felt I had a few seasons left in my bones.

It was not until the 1973 season began that I saw how drastically the team chemistry had started to change. It is inevitable, I suppose. Things move in and out of balance. In 1970 and '71 we had an offensive unit that was run mainly by the players. In 1972 this was less true. My own feeling had been that the coaches were taking over in areas that players had been handling pretty well. In 1973, when we began to get into some trouble, I found myself in a lot of disagreement about what the remedy should be. I felt we had gotten out of touch with what we could do best. We were going from pillar to post, and we had lost our personality as an offensive team, while we spent what seemed to me too much time imitating what *other* teams were doing, trying to figure out, say, how Dallas beat Miami, and incorporating two or three of their plays, rather than figuring how we could beat Miami using what we already had.

I am not saying that any one person was wrong. I don't want to be *blaming* someone else. There is too much of that in football as it is — quarterbacks blaming coaches, coaches blaming quarterbacks. The main thing is there were strong differences of opinion, complicated by the

225

fact that I was in a rather unusual position as a player. I was the same age as about half the guys on the staff. Take Paul Wiggin. He and I played together at Stanford and in the same East-West Game in 1957, and 1973 was his sixth year as defensive line coach with the 49ers. I had more playing time in than anyone else around. I had more on-field experience than about 95 percent of the people who have ever played the game. It isn't surprising that this could lead to some friction if I had a theory that ran up against a theory being offered by one of the coaches. When you're in high school and college, you sort of need the fatherly attitude a lot of coaches take toward their players. When you are just out of college and anxious to make it in the pros, you take what they give you. But the more you know, or think you know, the less you blindly accept, the harder you look at things, the solider your own theories are in regard to what works and doesn't work.

I had been on losing teams and on winning teams, and I thought I understood the differences. In 1973 I started seeing things happening to the 49ers that I couldn't do enough about. I could see it because I had watched so many different combinations. But I couldn't do enough about it because I was still a player. My main job was still to go out there on weekends and throw the football. I couldn't contribute as much as I thought I was capable of. In the dynamics of what goes on between players and coaches, things had sort of reached a breaking point: my experience was in excess of my position within the organization. It finally got to where I was either going to have to have more say in the way things were running, or shut up and be satisfied to sit on the bench if that was what the coaches thought was best for the team, or leave the organization.

Well, I had been through all this before. It was a kind of battle I didn't really want to fight again. I had been through four head coaches. I guess I had developed a sense for the rhythm of things. The chemistry, which had been ideal in 1970, had shifted. The ingredients were out of balance. Something had to give. In 1967 it had been the coach who finally left, and I had found the enthusiasm to start over, with myself, and with the team. Under Dick Nolan I had the three most enjoyable football seasons of my career. But by 1973 my mind was in a different place. I saw later that this in itself affected my performance on the field. That, in turn, added another wrinkle. It kept me out of some ball games. The only reason I had ever suited up was in order to play. None of it was worth the bother if I couldn't play and if it wasn't fun when I did.

There came a point, midway through the season, when Nolan decided to start Steve Spurrier in a game against Atlanta. I was miffed, no doubt about it, because the previous week Steve had started and the team wasn't doing too well, and after I went in during the second quarter and played out the game, we beat them, 40-0. It was said that Dick's decision to start Spurrier against Atlanta the next weekend "forced" me into retirement, because the same day he made that announcement, I announced I was quitting. It was not at all that cut and dried. All these other things were feeding in at once to create that decision. When the time came it wasn't really very hard to make. I had other fish to fry. I had played enough football for one lifetime. I was ready to move on.

An Open Field

FOOTBALL IS OFTEN ATTACKED these days for its commercialism, for having become an enormous product packaged by the major networks and the oil companies and sold to a nation of consumers like six-packs of beer. That is one way to look at the game, all right. From a player's point of view, if that's the only way you see it, the sport will overwhelm you; you will end up hating football and hating yourself for playing it.

I always tried to keep focused on the game itself, what was happening on the field, not in the office buildings or on the TV screen between quarters or on the sports pages between games. I can honestly say now that this game allowed me to grow a great deal as a human being. I am not the only player who will say so. But it is a viewpoint that seems to get lost the more profitable the game becomes and the more attacks that are leveled against it.

It seems wonderful to me now, with all the experience I have had, to be able to gain enough awareness about the game and through the game to be prepared to do something else, to make my own decision to go into other areas of life and to be happy I was able to play that game as long as I did.

The last time I suited up with the 49ers, they staged a John Brodie Day at Candlestick Park. I didn't think too much about it beforehand. My mind was on the game. Suddenly there I was at a microphone down on the sidelines, and it started to well up inside of me, the whole idea of having to say goodby to sixty thousand people. They may not have been the same sixty thousand I started out with, but for that moment it was like they had been coming out there every weekend for seventeen years to watch us move the ball around. I was glad to be able to thank them for the whole trip. My throat got tight. I had to make it short before I started bawling right there on the field.

Then I kind of put it all out of my mind again while we went ahead and played.

It wasn't until afterward that it really hit me, the fact that I would never be warming up again, or playing again, or unwinding after the game — that it was all over. As I was leaving the field, I noticed that someone had lit up the lights on Candlestick's electric scoreboard, so that it read, THE END OF AN ERA. Glancing at that I thought, "What the hell is *this?*" I walked on into the dressing room, showered and changed, and then went out to the parking lot where Sue and the kids were waiting in the car.

By that time the kids weren't much concerned about the outcome of the game, or the season, or anything but where we were going to go eat dinner. I don't remember what was decided. I didn't really hear the conversation. As we were driving out of the parking lot at Candlestick, the electric scoreboard flashed into my mind again. This time, the finality of those words convinced me that something definitely had come to a close. Something personal. That's how I read it anyway. An era in *my* life. But it wasn't as if I were just adrift and floating around looking for another place to land. The next era had already begun.

I already had one foot firmly planted in this new field before I had taken the last step off the gridiron, which was a rather small and narrow field by comparison. The one I had stepped out into was wide open, and I felt good about it. I was in motion. I was ready for anything.